Absolutely Every[*]

BED & BREAKFAST

[*]Almost

SOUTHERN CALIFORNIA

EDITED BY CARL HANSON

SASQUATCH BOOKS
SEATTLE

Printed in the United States of America.
Distributed in Canada by Raincoast Books Ltd.
03 02 01 00 99   5 4 3 2 1

Cover design: Jane Jeszeck
Cover illustration: Eric Meola/The Image Bank
Interior design and composition: Alan Bernhard
Editor: Carl Hanson
Copy editors: Diane Sepanski, Christine Clifton-Thornton

ISSN 1522-5488
ISBN 1-57061-193-9

Sasquatch Books
615 Second Avenue
Seattle, Washington 98104
(206) 467-4300
books@SasquatchBooks.com
http://www.SasquatchBooks.com

CONTENTS

ABSOLUTELY EVERY BED & BREAKFAST SERIES

Welcome to *Absolutely Every° Bed & Breakfast: Southern California (°Almost)*, a comprehensive guide to virtually every bed and breakfast establishment in Southern California. We've done the work for you: Everything you need to know in choosing a bed and breakfast is included on these pages, from architectural style to atmosphere, from price range to breakfast variety. Listings are in alphabetical order by town, so locating the perfect stay at your destination is a snap, and the simple format makes comparing accommodations as easy as turning the page. So whether you're looking for an elegant Victorian inn, a stunning chateau in the heart of wine country, or a cozy seaside cottage, *Absolutely Every° Bed & Breakfast: Southern California (°Almost)* will help you find it.

In addition to Southern California, the *Absolutely Every* series covers Arizona, Colorado, New Mexico, Northern California, Oregon, Washington, and Texas; look for the latest edition of each in your local bookstore. The guides list small- and medium-sized inns, hotels, and host homes that include breakfast in the price of the room. The lists of B&B establishments are compiled from a variety of sources, including directories, chambers of commerce, tourism bureaus, and the World Wide Web. After gathering a complete list, the editors send each innkeeper a survey, asking for basic lodging information and for those special details that set them apart. The completed surveys are then examined and fact-checked for accuracy before inclusion in the book. The °*Almost* in the series title reflects the fact that a small number of innkeepers may choose not to be listed, may neglect to respond to the survey and follow-up phone calls, or are not listed because of negative reports received by the editors.

The editors rely on the honesty of the innkeepers in completing the surveys and on feedback from readers to keep the *Absolutely Every Bed & Breakfast* series accurate and up-to-date. (*Note:* While innkeepers are responsible for providing survey information, none are financially connected to the series, nor do they pay any fees to be included in the book.) Please° write to us about your experience at any of the bed and breakfasts listed in the series; we'd love to hear from you.

Enjoy your bed and breakfast experience!

—The editors, *Absolutely Every Bed & Breakfast*

HOW TO USE THIS BOOK

Absolutely Every Bed & Breakfast: Southern California is organized alphabetically by town and by establishment name, and includes a comprehensive index. The concise, at-a-glance format of the complete bed and breakfast listings covers fifteen categories of information to help you select just the right bed and breakfast accommodation for your needs. This edition offers you a choice of establishments in cities, towns, and outlying areas.

THE BED & BREAKFAST LISTINGS

Note that although specifics of each establishment have been confirmed by the editors, details such as amenities, decor, and breakfast menus have been provided by the innkeepers. Listings in this guide are subject to change; call to confirm all aspects of your stay, including price, availability, and restrictions, before you go. Some bed and breakfast listings offer only selected information due to lack of response or by request of the innkeeper; complete listings include the following information.

Establishment name
Address: Note that street addresses often vary from actual mailing addresses; confirm the mailing address before sending a reservation payment.
Telephone numbers: Includes any toll-free or fax numbers.
Innkeeper's languages: Languages spoken other than English.
Location: Directions from the nearest town, highway, or landmark.
Open: Notice of any seasonal or other closures.
Description: Overview of architecture, furnishings, landscaping, etc.
Rooms: Number of rooms with private bathrooms vs. shared baths; availability of suites and/or additional guesthouses; and the innkeeper's favorite room.
Rates: Range of room prices, which vary based on private or shared bathroom, season, and individual room amenities. Also noted here are any minimum stay requirements and cancellation policies (usually two weeks' notice is required for a full refund).

Breakfast: Description of breakfast served (full, continental, continental plus, or stocked kitchen).

Credit cards: Indicates which, if any, credit cards are accepted. Note that credit cards may be listed for reservation confirmation purposes only; be prepared to pay by check or cash.

Amenities: Details any special amenities that are included.

Restrictions: Lists any restrictions regarding smoking, children, and pets. Also listed here are any resident pets or livestock.

Awards: Any significant hospitality or historic preservation awards received.

Reviewed: Publications in which the B&B has been reviewed.

Rated: Indicates whether the B&B has been rated by institutions such as the American Automobile Association (AAA), American Bed & Breakfast Association (ABBA), or the Mobil Travel Association.

Member: Indicates membership in any professional hospitality associations or organizations.

Kudos/Comments: Comments from guests who have stayed in the establishment.

ALPINE

Twenty-eight miles from downtown San Diego, the village of Alpine is nestled in the foothills of the Viejas Mountains. You can gamble or play bingo 24 hours a day at the Viejas Casino & Turf Club.

CEDAR CREEK INN

Alpine, CA   *619-445-9605*

VICTORIA ROCK BED & BREAKFAST

2952 North Victoria Drive, Alpine, CA 91901   *619-659-5967*
Helga & Darrel Doliber, Innkeepers
German spoken
WEBSITE *www.victoria-rock-bb.com*

OPEN	All year
DESCRIPTION	A Mediterranean-style host home with a red-tile roof, situated on 3 acres on the slopes of the Viejas Mountains.
NO. OF ROOMS	Four suites with private bathrooms.
RATES	Year-round rates are $80-100 for a single or double. Cancellation requires seven days' notice.
CREDIT CARDS	MasterCard, Visa
BREAKFAST	Full gourmet breakfast is served in the dining room.
AMENITIES	Spa, steam room, and sauna; fireplaces in three rooms; one room with a Jacuzzi tub; wedding and reception facilities; air conditioning; bird-watching; hammocks; telescope for stargazing; interior courtyard; two rooms with private patio and garden.
RESTRICTIONS	No smoking, no pets, accommodations are not suitable for children.

ARROWHEAD

ROSE GABLES BED & BREAKFAST

Arrowhead, CA   909-336-9892

ARROYO GRANDE

The Edna Valley region is a lush and gorgeous viticultural area, producing some of California's best wines. Tour the vineyards, taste the wines, and be there for the annual Harvest Celebration on Veteran's Day Weekend. Don't miss the coastal sand dunes along the stretch between Pismo Beach and Oceano. Check out the Strawberry Festival over Memorial Day Weekend and ooooh and aaaaaah over the fireworks shot off the Pismo Beach pier on July 4th. About 10 miles southeast of San Luis Obispo via Highway 101.

ARROYO VILLAGE INN BED & BREAKFAST

407 El Camino Real, Arroyo Grande, CA 93420   805-489-5926
Gina Glass, Innkeeper   800-563-7762
Italian and Spanish spoken
WEBSITE *www.centralcoast.com/arroyovillageinn*

LOCATION	From Highway 101 north, exit at Brisco Road, take a left at the stop, then another left on El Camino Real. From Highway 101 south, take the Halcyon exit and go left on Camino Real.
OPEN	All year
DESCRIPTION	A 1984 three-story English farmhouse decorated with Laura Ashley prints and antiques.
NO. OF ROOMS	Seven rooms with private bathrooms.
RATES	Year-round rates are $135-375 for a suite. There is a minimum stay over holidays and during special events. Inquire about a cancellation policy.
CREDIT CARDS	American Express, Diners Club, Discover, MasterCard, Visa
BREAKFAST	Full gourmet breakfast or brunch is served in the dining room and includes only natural ingredients.

AMENITIES	In-room spas and fireplaces; sitting areas; window seats; skylights; 24-hour complimentary wines, cordials, and teas; snacks on busy weekends; robes in spa rooms; chocolates and candies in rooms; candles in all rooms; champagne or homemade birthday cake for celebrations.
RESTRICTIONS	No smoking, no pets. Inquire about children.

CRYSTAL ROSE INN

789 Valley Road, Arroyo Grande, CA 93420   *805-481-1854*
EMAIL *stay@crystalroseinn*   *800-Rose-Inn*
WEBSITE *www.centralcoast.com/crystalroseinn*

LOCATION	Five minutes from Pismo Beach.
OPEN	All year
DESCRIPTION	A renovated 1890 two-story Victorian inn, carriage house, and cottage, decorated with period antiques and reproductions, situated on 1.5 acres of rose and herb gardens.
NO. OF ROOMS	Eight rooms with private bathrooms.
RATES	Please inquire about current rates. Special packages and corporate rates are available. Cancellation requires seven days' notice.
CREDIT CARDS	American Express, Discover, MasterCard, Visa
BREAKFAST	Full gourmet breakfast is served in the tea room by candlelight, or in the garden or guestrooms.
AMENITIES	On-site restaurant, afternoon high tea, evening wine and hors d'oeuvres, complimentary newspaper, gazebo, patio, on-site massage therapist, wedding facilities, amenities for the business traveler (telephones, fax, copier, data ports, audio/visual equipment, meeting facilities).
REVIEWED	*National Geographic* magazine

GRIEB FARMHOUSE INN

851 Todd Lane, Arroyo Grande, CA 93420   *805-481-8540*
EMAIL *info@griebfarmhouseinn.com*
WEBSITE *www.griebfarmhouseinn.com*

LOCATION	Eighty-five miles north of Santa Barbara, 12 miles from San Luis Obispo, and 2 miles from Pismo Beach.

OPEN	All year
DESCRIPTION	A restored 1888 two-story farmhouse decorated with charming country decor.
RATES	Please inquire about current rates. There is a two-night minimum stay during weekends and holidays. Cancellation requires 48 hours' notice.
BREAKFAST	Full gourmet breakfast is served
AMENITIES	Evening refreshments, morning coffee and tea service, gardens, porches.
AWARDS	1998, Beautification Award, Arroyo Grande Chamber of Commerce

THE GUEST HOUSE

120 Hart Lane, Arroyo Grande, CA 93420   805-481-9304
Mark Miller & Jim Cunningham, Innkeepers

LOCATION	Halfway between Los Angeles and San Francisco, 2 blocks off Highway 101.
OPEN	All year
DESCRIPTION	An 1865 pre-Victorian decorated with antiques, located in the heart of the historic village.
NO. OF ROOMS	Two rooms share one bathroom.
RATES	Year-round rates are $50-70 for a single or double. Ask about a cancellation policy.
CREDIT CARDS	No
BREAKFAST	Full breakfast is served in the dining room and includes fresh fruit, juice, a hot dish, rolls, and coffee or tea.
AMENITIES	Afternoon tea and snacks.
RESTRICTIONS	No pets. Children over 10 are welcome. Hana is the resident Siamese cat.

HOUSE OF ANOTHER TYME BED & BREAKFAST

227 Le Point Street, Arroyo Grande, CA 93420   805-489-6313
Jack & Judy, Innkeepers   FAX 805-489-6313
WEBSITE *www.virtualcities.com*

LOCATION	From Highway 101, take the Grand Avenue exit and head east 0.5 mile to the light at Mason Street. Turn left and drive up the hill 1 block to Le Point Street. The B&B is straight ahead.
OPEN	All year
DESCRIPTION	A 1916 two-story simple Victorian of single-wall construction decorated with antiques and situated on 0.25 acre.
NO. OF ROOMS	Three rooms with private bathrooms.
RATES	Year-round rates are $95 for a single or double. There is no minimum stay and cancellation requires three days' notice.
CREDIT CARDS	Discover, MasterCard, Visa
BREAKFAST	Full breakfast is served in the dining room and includes fruit cup, a hot dish such as quiche or French toast, bacon or sausage, smoothie, muffins, breakfast cake, coffee, tea, or milk.
AMENITIES	Coffee or tea with cake or cookies in the afternoon, patio, sun porch, exotic finches, koi pond.
RESTRICTIONS	No smoking, no pets, children over 16 are welcome. Disney and Pumpkin are the resident cats. There are also fish in the koi pond, and finches. All are outdoor animals.

ATASCADERO

LAKE VIEW BED & BREAKFAST

9065 Lake View Drive, Atascadero, CA 93422   805-466-5665
Lee Swam, Innkeeper

AVALON

Avalon is a community of singular beauty at the southeastern edge of Santa Catalina Island, California's "Isle of Eternal Spring," so named because the temperature hovers perpetually within a few notches of 70-degrees Fahrenheit. A main attraction here is the Undersea Museum. Local celebrations include the Catalina Island Blues Festival and Silent Film Benefit in May and the Catalina Wine and Surf Music Festivals in September. Home tours, art and jazz festivals, and runs of all sizes (including triathlons, marathons, and the daunting Catalina 100K) take place throughout the year. Two passenger ferries serve Avalon: one disembarks from Long Beach, the other from Newport Beach. For those in a hurry, jet helicopters shuttle passengers between Avalon and Long Beach.

BANNING HOUSE LODGE

1 Banning House Road, Avalon, CA 90704　　　　　　　　　*310-510-2800*
WEBSITE www.catalina.com/twoharbors/mainlodging.html

OPEN	All Year
DESCRIPTION	A 1910 lodge perched above the village of Two Harbors.
NO. OF ROOMS	Eleven rooms with private bathrooms. Cabins are also available.
RATES	Please inquire about current rates and cancellation information.
CREDIT CARDS	American Express, Diners Club, Discover, MasterCard, Visa
BREAKFAST	Continental breakfast is served in the dining room.
AMENITIES	Free shuttle service between the lodge and Two Harbors village; rooms have partial-to-full water views.
RESTRICTIONS	No smoking, no pets

CATALINA ISLAND INN

125 Metropole Avenue, Avalon, CA 90704　　　　　　　　　*310-510-1624*
EMAIL islinn@catalinas.net

LOCATION	Half a block from the beach at Avalon.
RATES	Year-round rates are $100-219 for a single or double and $250 for a minisuite. There are special packages and midweek discounts during spring and winter.
BREAKFAST	Continental breakfast is served.
AMENITIES	Cable TV, telephones, balconies with beautiful harbor views.

CATALINA ISLAND SEACREST INN

201 Claressa Avenue, Avalon, CA 90704   *310-510-0800*
EMAIL *info@catalinas.net*   *FAX 310-510-1122*
WEBSITE *www.catalina.com/seacrest.html*

LOCATION	One block from the beach in Avalon.
DESCRIPTION	A two-story inn with Victorian decor.
RATES	Please inquire about current rates. Special packages are available. There is a two-night minimum stay during most weekends, and cancellation requires seven days' notice.
CREDIT CARDS	American Express, MasterCard, Visa
BREAKFAST	Continental breakfast is served in the sun room.
AMENITIES	Some rooms have electric fireplaces, most rooms have whirlpools or tubs for two, queen- or king-size canopy or four-poster beds, cable TV with movie channels, video library.
REVIEWED	*Romantic Southern California*
MEMBER	Professional Association of Innkeepers International

THE INN ON MOUNT ADA

398 Wrigley Road, Avalon, CA 90704   *310-510-2030*
WEBSITE *www.catalina.com/mtada*   *800-608-7669*

OPEN	All year
DESCRIPTION	An elegant 1921 two-story mansion perched atop Mount Ada, 350 feet above the harbor with spectacular views of the ocean and harbor.
NO. OF ROOMS	Five rooms and one suite with private bathrooms.
RATES	Please inquire about current rates. A two-night minimum stay is required during weekends and holidays; and cancellation requires ten days' notice with a $50 fee.
CREDIT CARDS	MasterCard, Visa
BREAKFAST	Full breakfast is served in the dining room. A light lunch is also included.
AMENITIES	Four rooms with fireplaces; all rooms have ocean or harbor views; appetizers, fresh-baked cookies, fresh fruit, soft drinks, beer, wine, and champagne.

RESTRICTIONS   No smoking, no pets, children over 14 are welcome.

KUDOS/COMMENTS   "Beautiful hilltop mansion overlooking the bay. Relaxing
                    atmosphere and superior views."

OLD TURNER INN

232 Catalina Avenue, Avalon, CA 90704   *310-510-2236*
WEBSITE *www.catalina.com/Old_Turner_Inn/index.html*

LOCATION   One block from the beach.

OPEN   All year

DESCRIPTION   A renovated 1927 Cape Cod inn decorated with English and
                   American antiques.

NO. OF ROOMS   Five rooms with private bathrooms.

RATES   Please inquire about current rates and cancellation information.

BREAKFAST   Full breakfast is served in the sun porch and includes fresh fruit,
                   homemade granola, yogurt, fresh-baked goods, pastries, and a main
                   dish.

AMENITIES   Evening wine and appetizers; four rooms with wood-burning
                   fireplaces; all rooms with queen- or king-size beds; bicycles.

ZANE GREY PUEBLO HOTEL

199 Chimes Tower Road, Avalon, CA 90704   *310-510-0966*
Karen Baker, Innkeeper
Spanish spoken
WEBSITE *www.bbchannel.com/bbc/p213410.asp*

LOCATION   On Catalina Island, 22 miles off the coast of Los Angeles.

OPEN   All year

DESCRIPTION   A 1926 Hopi pueblo-style inn overlooking Avalon Casino. The hotel
                   was built by Zane Grey.

NO. OF ROOMS   Eighteen rooms with private bathrooms.

RATES   Please inquire about current rates and cancellation information.

CREDIT CARDS   American Express, MasterCard, Visa

BREAKFAST   Continental breakfast is served.

AMENITIES	Swimming pool with surrounding deck, beach, snorkeling, scuba diving, boating, golf, tennis, horseback riding, parasailing, shuttle service from the ferry dock.
RESTRICTIONS	No smoking indoors, no pets, children are welcome. There is a resident cat.

BALLARD
(SOLVANG)

This little hamlet in Santa Ynez Valley features the charming little red Ballard Schoolhouse, in continuous use since 1883. Celebrate the grape during one of Ballard's many wine festivals or take a taste from any of 50 local wineries. For outdoor fun, Ballard is handy to Lake Cachuma Recreation Area. From Santa Barbara, about 27 miles northwest via Highway 154, 50 miles via Highway 101.

BALLARD INN

2436 Baseline Avenue, Ballard, CA 93463
Larry Stone & Steve Hyslop, Innkeepers
Spanish spoken
EMAIL *innkeeper@ballardinn.com*

805-688-7770
800-638-2466
FAX 805-688-9560
WEBSITE *www.ballardinn.com*

LOCATION	From Highway 101, take the Solvang exit and follow Route 246 east through Solvang to Alamo Pintado Road. Turn left, drive 3 miles to Baseline Avenue, and turn right.
OPEN	All year
DESCRIPTION	A 1984 two-story country inn with rooms that reflect local history, located in the heart of Santa Barbara wine country.
NO. OF ROOMS	Fifteen rooms with private bathrooms.
RATES	Year-round rates are $170-250 for a single or double. There is a two-night minimum stay on weekends and holidays, and cancellation requires seven days' notice, 30 days for groups.
CREDIT CARDS	American Express, MasterCard, Visa
BREAKFAST	Full breakfast cooked to order is served in the dining room and includes four entrée selections.
AMENITIES	Wine and hors d'oeuvres, home-baked cookies, fresh flowers, special packages, Cafe Chardonnay serves creative wine-country cuisine.
RESTRICTIONS	No smoking, no pets

REVIEWED	*The Best Places to Kiss in Southern California, Weekends for Two in Southern California*
MEMBER	International Innkeepers Association, Professional Association of Innkeepers International, California Association of Bed & Breakfast Inns
RATED	AAA 4 Diamonds, Best Places to Kiss 4 Lips, Mobil 3 Stars

BAYWOOD PARK
(MORRO BAY)

Nestled on the coast just south of Morro Bay, Baywood Park was once named Valley of the Bears by Spanish explorers because of the abundance of grizzlies. So be on the lookout! Splendid Montana de Oro State Park is only 10 miles southwest.

BAYWOOD BED & BREAKFAST INN

1370 2nd Street, Baywood Park, CA 93402   805-528-8888
Pat & Alex Benson, Innkeepers   805-528-8887
Spanish and French spoken
EMAIL *innkeeper@baywoodinn.com*
WEBSITE *www.baywoodinn.com*

LOCATION	On Morro Bay, 10 miles northwest of San Luis Obispo.
OPEN	All year
DESCRIPTION	A large contemporary inn with theme rooms.
NO. OF ROOMS	Fifteen rooms with private bathrooms.
RATES	Year-round rates are $80-160 for a single or double. Cancellation requires five days' notice.
CREDIT CARDS	MasterCard, Visa
BREAKFAST	Full gourmet breakfast is served in the dining room or guestrooms and includes fresh-squeezed juice, locally grown fruits and vegetables, homemade muffins, preserves, and eggs.
AMENITIES	Scenic bay views; private entrances; queen-size beds, fireplaces, microwaves, telephones, radios, TVs, hair dryers, refrigerator in every room; boat launch; pier; canoeing, kayaking, small boat sailing, hiking, bicycling, bird-watching; evening wine, cheese, hors d'oeuvres, and room tours; facilities for meetings, reunions, and private parties; one suite is handicapped accessible.
RESTRICTIONS	No smoking, no pets

REVIEWED   *Los Angeles* magazine

RATED   ABBA 3 Crowns

BIG BEAR
(BIG BEAR CITY & BIG BEAR LAKE)

Big Bear is the ideal place for a quick, cool alpine escape from the cities and deserts of south-central California. Summer activities center around the 7-mile-long lake. In winter, choose from three nearby ski resorts. Celebrate Oktoberfest in grand style in the fall. From San Bernardino, 30 miles east via I-215 and Highway 330.

ALPENHORN BED & BREAKFAST

601 Knight Avenue, Big Bear Lake, CA 92315   909-866-8221
Chuck & Robbie Slemaker, Innkeepers   888-829-6600
WEBSITE *www.alpenhorn.com*   FAX 909-878-3209

LOCATION	Midway between the village and the Snow Summit ski area.
OPEN	All year
DESCRIPTION	A modern mountain home with luxurious, comfortable furnishings, situated on 1 forested acre.
NO. OF ROOMS	Seven rooms with private bathrooms.
RATES	Year-round weekend rates are $135-185 for a single or double. Midweek rates are slightly less. There is a two-night minimum stay on weekends, and cancellation requires 72 hours' notice.
CREDIT CARDS	American Express, Discover, MasterCard, Visa
BREAKFAST	Full gourmet breakfast is served in the dining room and includes homemade granola, yogurt, breads, fresh seasonal fruit, a hot entrée, juices, coffee, and tea.
AMENITIES	King- or queen-size beds, hypoallergenic featherbeds; robes; luxurious spa towels; basket with Aveda products and vanity kit; fireplace, spa tubs, digital telephones in rooms; TV/VCR; private balconies; fresh flowers; cookies, coffee, tea, ice tea, lemonade available all day long, evening hors d'oeuvres and wine; See's chocolates and a variety of after-dinner liqueurs; gazebo.
RESTRICTIONS	No smoking, no pets
MEMBER	Professional Association of Innkeepers International

APPLES BED & BREAKFAST INN

42430 Moonridge Road, Big Bear Lake, CA 92315   **909-866-0903**
Jim & Barbara McLean, Innkeepers
WEBSITE *www.bigbear.com/apples*

LOCATION	From Los Angeles, take I-10 east to Route 30, then north to Route 330. Follow Route 330/18 to Big Bear Lake. Turn right at the dam and follow the highway to the stop sign in the village. Turn left on Pinknot Road, right on Big Bear Boulevard, and right again on Moonridge Road. The inn is 0.5 mile on the left.
OPEN	All year
DESCRIPTION	A 1992 two-story country Victorian inn, designed and built by the owners on a landscaped wooded acre within the San Bernardino National Forest. The inn is decorated with country Victorian furnishings.
NO. OF ROOMS	Twelve rooms with private bathrooms. Try the Red Delicious Room.
RATES	Year-round rates are $130-225 for a single or double. There is a two-night minimum stay on weekends, and cancellation requires seven days' notice.
CREDIT CARDS	American Express, Discover, MasterCard, Visa
BREAKFAST	Full breakfast is served in the dining room and includes French toast with apple-peach syrup, herb and cheese scrambled eggs, honey-apple sausage, pineapple-cranberry bran muffins, juice, tea, and coffee.
AMENITIES	Afternoon sparkling cider and cheese; evening dessert and snack bar; each room has a gas fireplace, TV/VCR, recliners, king-size beds with down bedding, apple-scented bath gel soap and shampoo, and hair dryers; bottled water; hot tub; paddle tennis court, basketball, and hammocks.
RESTRICTIONS	No smoking, no pets. Two people per room only.
REVIEWED	*Fodor's California's Best Bed & Breakfasts, The Best Places to Kiss in Southern California, Romantic Big Bear*
MEMBER	California Lodging Industry Association

CAROLYN'S COTTAGE BED & BREAKFAST

42728 Cougar Road, Big Bear Lake, CA 92315   909-584-2467
Bob & Julie Walsh, Innkeepers   FAX 909-584-0054
Spanish spoken
EMAIL *info@carolynscottage.com*
WEBSITE *www.carolynscottage.com*

OPEN	All year
DESCRIPTION	A two-story Victorian-style cottage located in a quiet residential neighborhood near Bear Mountain and Snow Summit ski resorts.
NO. OF ROOMS	Three rooms with private bathrooms.
RATES	High-season rates are $98-185 for a single or double. Off-season rates are $75-155. There is a two-night minimum stay during holidays, and cancellation requires one week's notice with a fee.
CREDIT CARDS	American Express, MasterCard, Visa
BREAKFAST	Full gourmet breakfast is served in the dining room and may include stuffed French toast or Belgian waffles.
AMENITIES	Fresh flowers; homemade cookies; TV/VCR in rooms; living room with fireplace; ice tea, lemonade, and apple cider available all day; king- or queen-size beds; robes; hosts provide extras for special occasions.
RESTRICTIONS	No smoking, no pets. Maximum of two guests per room. Tiberius is the orange cat; Chili is the calico. Sheena is the cocker spaniel; the English springer spaniel is Shasta.
MEMBER	California Association of Bed & Breakfast Inns

CATHY'S COUNTRY COTTAGES

600 W Big Bear Boulevard, Big Bear City, CA 92314   909-866-7444
John & Tracy Green, Innkeepers   800-544-7454
EMAIL *Cathy@CathysCottages.com*   WEBSITE *www.cathyscottages.com*

LOCATION	Approximately 3 miles east of Big Bear Lake on Highway 18 at Blue Water. Big Bear Lake is 100 miles east of Los Angeles. Take I-10 east to Highway 30 north, to Highway 330 north, to Highway 18 north.
OPEN	All year
DESCRIPTION	A romantic 1945 two-story cottage with Victorian country decor. The Hitching Post wedding chapel is on site.

NO. OF ROOMS	Six rooms with private bathrooms.
RATES	Year-round weekend and holiday rates are $79-199 for a single or double. Midweek rates are $49-149. There is a minimum stay during weekends and holidays, and cancellation requires 15 days' notice.
CREDIT CARDS	American Express, Diners Club, Discover, MasterCard, Visa
BREAKFAST	Continental breakfast is served in the guestrooms and includes fruit, Danish, bagel, juice, coffee, and tea.
AMENITIES	Jacuzzi, fireplace, dual showerheads, wet bar, robes, private cabins.
RESTRICTIONS	No smoking, no pets, no children
RATED	AAA 3 Diamonds

EAGLE'S NEST BED & BREAKFAST

41675 Big Bear Boulevard, Big Bear Lake, CA 92315   909-866-6465

GOLD MOUNTAIN MANOR HISTORIC B&B

1117 Anita Avenue, Big Bear Lake, CA 92314   909-585-6997
Jose Tapia, Innkeeper   800-509-2604
Spanish spoken   FAX 909-585-0327
EMAIL *goldmtn@bigbear.com*   WEBSITE *www.bigbear.com/goldmtn*

LOCATION	Two miles east of Big Bear Village across the Stainfield Cutoff.
OPEN	All year
DESCRIPTION	A 1928 two-story log mansion with a rock fireplace and furnished in antiques, set on an acre of pine trees, half a block from the National Forest. Listed on the State Historic Register.
NO. OF ROOMS	Seven rooms with private bathrooms. Try the Ted Ducey Suite.
RATES	Year-round rates are $125-149 for a single or double, $180-190 for a suite, and $175-250 for the guesthouse. There is a minimum stay on weekends and holidays, and cancellation requires seven days' notice.
CREDIT CARDS	American Express, Discover, MasterCard, Visa
BREAKFAST	Full breakfast is served in the dining room, guestrooms, or on the veranda and includes blueberry granola pancakes with fresh blueberries and buttermilk batter.

AMENITIES	Large den with big-screen TV; library; guest kitchen stocked with coffee, teas, and baked goods all day; robes; wood-burning fireplaces.
RESTRICTIONS	No smoking, no pets, no children, no hard liquor. Oliver and Shane are the resident Labs.
REVIEWED	*The Best Places to Kiss in Southern California*, *L.A.* magazine, *Sunset* magazine, *Outside* magazine, *50 Most Romantic Places in Southern California*, *Westways* magazine
MEMBER	Professional Association of Innkeepers International
RATED	AAA 3 Diamonds, Mobil 3 Stars
KUDOS/COMMENTS	"Historic log mansion, romantic rooms with wood-burning fireplaces, charming hosts, excellent service."

KNICKERBOCKER MANSION

43113 Moonridge Road, Big Bear Lake, CA 92315   *909-585-6914*
EMAIL *knickmail@aol.com*   *877-423-1180*
WEBSITE *www.knickerbockermansion.com*   *FAX 909-878-4248*

LOCATION	Three blocks from the village, 4 blocks from the lake.
OPEN	All year
DESCRIPTION	A rustic 1920 three-story log lodge and carriage house.
NO. OF ROOMS	Nine rooms and two suites with private bathrooms.
RATES	Please inquire about current rates. There is a two-night minimum stay on weekends, three nights during most major holidays. Cancellation requires seven days' notice, 14 days during holidays.
CREDIT CARDS	American Express, Discover, MasterCard, Visa
BREAKFAST	Full gourmet breakfast is served.
AMENITIES	All rooms with queen-size beds, telephones, TV/VCRs; afternoon refreshments; specialty coffee, tea, and other beverages are available all day; one room is handicapped accessible.
RESTRICTIONS	No smoking, no pets

MOONRIDGE MANOR BED & BREAKFAST

43803 Yosemite Drive, Big Bear Lake, CA 92315   909-585-0457
WEBSITE www.moonridge.com

OPEN	All year
DESCRIPTION	A three-story New England manor with traditional decor, situated in the San Bernardino National Forest, with views of ski slopes and mountains.
NO. OF ROOMS	Three rooms with private bathrooms and two rooms share a bath.
RATES	Please inquire about current rates, midweek discounts, and cancellation information.
CREDIT CARDS	American Express, MasterCard, Visa
BREAKFAST	Full gourmet breakfast is served.
AMENITIES	Discounted lift tickets to Snow Summit; library; greenhouse Jacuzzi; fireplace; the third-story suite features king-size bed, fireplace, whirlpool for two, and private balcony; homemade desserts.
RESTRICTIONS	No smoking, no pets

SWITZERLAND HAUS

41829 Switzerland Drive, Big Bear Lake, CA 92315   909-866-3729
Michael Harb, Innkeeper   800-335-3729
Arabic spoken
WEBSITE www.switzerlandhaus.com

OPEN	All year
DESCRIPTION	A Swiss-style host home.
NO. OF ROOMS	Five rooms with private bathrooms.
RATES	Please inquire about current rates and cancellation information.
CREDIT CARDS	Discover, MasterCard, Visa
BREAKFAST	Full breakfast is served in the dining room and includes coffee, tea, hot chocolate, juices, fresh fruit, and a hot dish such as French toast.
AMENITIES	TV/VCR, mountain views, afternoon refreshments, Nordic sauna, flower gardens, massages by appointment.
RESTRICTIONS	No smoking, no pets

TRUFFLES BED & BREAKFAST

43591 Bow Canyon Road, Big Bear Lake, CA 92315   909-585-2772
Marilyn Kane & Carol Kuhn Bracey, Innkeepers
WEBSITE www.bigbear.com/truffles

OPEN	All year
DESCRIPTION	A country manor decorated with traditional and antique furnishings, situated at 7,000 feet in the San Bernardino National Forest.
NO. OF ROOMS	Five rooms with private bathrooms.
RATES	Please inquire about current rates and cancellation information.
CREDIT CARDS	MasterCard, Visa
BREAKFAST	Full gourmet breakfast is served in the dining room and may include egg casseroles, quiche, or special French toast; plus bacon, breakfast potatoes, tea, coffee, and hot chocolate.
AMENITIES	Truffles on pillows at bedtime, featherbeds, library, conversation pit, exercise room, gift shop, afternoon teas, wedding facilities, late afternoon appetizer, evening dessert, homemade cookies, fireplace pit, mountain views.
RESTRICTIONS	No smoking, no pets, maximum of two guests per room.

BORREGO SPRINGS

Borrego Springs lies at the center of Anza-Borrego Desert State Park, a spectacular low-desert environment boasting geologic, geographic, and paleontologic jewels. The park also features bighorn sheep, and it is a perfect place for stargazing, with its clear, broad, ink-black skies. Borrego Springs is about 60 miles northeast of Escondido off Highway 78.

BORREGO VALLEY INN

405 Palm Canyon Drive, Borrego Springs, CA 92004   760-767-0311
Don & Mary Robidoux, Innkeepers   800-333-5810
Some Spanish spoken   FAX 760-767-0900
EMAIL borregovalleyinn1@Juno.com   *WEBSITE borregovalleyinn.com*

LOCATION	Half a mile west of Christmas Circle on Highway 522 in Borrego Springs.
OPEN	All year

DESCRIPTION	A 1998 southwestern/Santa Fe–style guesthouse with Sante Fe decor, set on 10 desert acres with magnificent views of Indian Head Mountain.
NO. OF ROOMS	Fourteen rooms with private bathrooms.
RATES	September through May, rates are $95-145 for a single or double. June through August, rates are $80-105 for a single or double. There is a minimum stay on weekends, and cancellation requires one week's notice.
CREDIT CARDS	American Express, Diners Club, Discover, MasterCard, Visa
BREAKFAST	Continental breakfast is served in the dining room and includes cereal, yogurt, sweet rolls, bagels, croissants, English muffins, dates, fruit bowl, and orange juice.
AMENITIES	Two pools, two spas, mountain bikes for rent, private patios and covered verandas, pedestal beds, Spanish-style showers, fireplaces in some rooms, barbecue facilities.
RESTRICTIONS	No smoking, no pets, children over 15 are welcome.

THE PALMS AT INDIAN HEAD

2220 Hoberg Road, Borrego Springs, CA 92004   760-767-7788
David Leibert, Innkeeper   800-519-2624
German and Spanish spoken   FAX 760-767-9717
EMAIL *thepalm1@juno.com*   WEBSITE *thepalmsatindianhead.com*

LOCATION	In Anza-Borrego Desert State Park, 2 hours from San Diego and 3 hours from Los Angeles. From the town center (Christmas Circle), go 3 miles west to Hoberg Road, then north 1 mile. "We are the only property on the left side of the road."
OPEN	All year
DESCRIPTION	A 1946 two-story art deco inn with Southwest lodgepole decor, a 20-acre hideaway for Hollywood stars in the '40s and '50s, located in Anza Borrego Desert State Park with spectacular views of Borrego Valley and Font's Point.
NO. OF ROOMS	Ten rooms with private bathrooms.
RATES	November through May, rates are $99-169 for a single or double. June through October, rates are $49-69 for a single or double. There is a minimum stay on weekends, and cancellation requires 72 hours' notice.
CREDIT CARDS	Diners Club, Discover, MasterCard, Visa
BREAKFAST	Continental plus is served in the dining room and includes yogurt, cereal, fruit, muffins, coffee, and orange juice. Lunch and dinner are also available.

AMENITIES	Spa, larger-than-Olympic-size pool, restaurant, panoramic view of Borrego Valley, turndown treats in rooms, meeting and wedding facilities, private dining rooms available, entire facility air conditioned. In season, guests are treated to an evening drink at the bar.
RESTRICTIONS	No smoking, no pets, children over 12 are welcome. Molly is the resident fox terrier. "She does not like children."
REVIEWED	*Sunset* magazine; *Los Angeles* magazine; *Frommer's; Off the Beaten Path; Lonely Planet; America's Favorite Inns, B&Bs and Small Hotels*
MEMBER	California Association of Bed & Breakfast Inns
AWARDS	1995, 1997, 1999, Hammer and Saw Award, Borrego Springs Chamber of Commerce

CAMBRIA

Its rugged coastline, pine forests, and vantage points for viewing annual whale migrations are prime reasons to visit this charming Victorian village. Established in the 1860s as a sea port, Cambria is now a thriving artists' colony. Close by are several wineries, and just six miles to the south is the famous Hearst Castle. Cambria is 35 miles north of San Luis Obispo on Highway 1.

A SUMMER PLACE

PO Box 1516, Cambria, CA 93428   *805-927-8145*
Don & Desi D'Urbano, Innkeepers
WEBSITE *sabre.bbchannel.com/bbc/p500190.asp*

OPEN	All year
DESCRIPTION	A 1950 Cape Cod–style host home in a wooded, coastal setting.
NO. OF ROOMS	One room with a private bathroom.
RATES	Year-round rates are $35-65 for a single or double. Ask about a cancellation policy.
CREDIT CARDS	No
BREAKFAST	Continental plus is served in the dining room.
AMENITIES	Excellent views, peace and quiet.
RESTRICTIONS	No smoking inside, no pets, children over 10 are welcome. There are three resident cats.

BEACH HOUSE

6360 *Moonstone Beach Drive, Cambria, CA 93428*   805-927-3136
WEBSITE www.moonstonebeach.com

BEACH HOUSE BED & BREAKFAST

6360 *Moonstone Beach Drive, Cambria, CA 93428*   805-927-3136
WEBSITE www.moonstonebeach.com

LOCATION	From Highway 1 north, pass through two stoplights in Cambria, turn left at the third, and then make a quick right onto Moonstone Beach Drive.
OPEN	All year
DESCRIPTION	A three-story A-frame beach house overlooking the water.
NO. OF ROOMS	Seven rooms with private bathrooms.
RATES	Year-round rates are $125-175 for a single or double. Cancellation requires seven days' notice.
CREDIT CARDS	MasterCard, Visa
BREAKFAST	Guests receive a coupon for breakfast at the Moonstone Beach Bar and Grill, where they can eat inside or on the patio facing the ocean.
AMENITIES	Living room with fireplace, library, TVs; binoculars and telescopes for viewing birds, seals, and whales; cozy fireplace on the second floor, oceanfront deck for watching the sunsets.
RESTRICTIONS	No pets
REVIEWED	*Sunset* magazine

BLUE WHALE INN

6736 Moonstone Beach Drive, Cambria, CA 93428   805-927-4647
Jan, Dave & John Crowther, Innkeepers   800-753-9000
Spanish spoken   FAX 805-927-4647
EMAIL *inkeeper@bluewhaleinn.com*   WEBSITE *www.bluewhaleinn.com*

LOCATION	From Highway 1, turn onto Windsor, then make an immediate right onto Moonstone Beach Drive. Go 0.25 mile; the B&B is on the right.
OPEN	All year
DESCRIPTION	A 1990 ranch-style inn with French country decor, situated across the road from the beach.
NO. OF ROOMS	Six rooms with private bathrooms.
RATES	Year-round rates are $190-250 for a single or double. There is a two- or three-night minimum stay on weekends and holidays, and cancellation requires 10 days' notice.
CREDIT CARDS	MasterCard, Visa
BREAKFAST	Full gourmet breakfast is served in the dining room. Continental plus is available for early risers.
AMENITIES	Afternoon tea and home-baked goods; cocktail hour with wine, cheese, and hors d'oeuvres; fireplace; canopy beds; partial views of the ocean from every room; private entrances.
RESTRICTIONS	No smoking, no pets, ask about children.
REVIEWED	*Karen Brown's California: Charming Inns & Itineraries*
MEMBER	California Commended Inns, California Association of Bed & Breakfast Inns
RATED	AAA 4 Diamonds, ABBA 4 Crowns

BURTON DRIVE INN

4036 Burton Drive, Cambria, CA 93428   805-927-5125
Bryan & Sylvia Hume, Innkeepers   FAX 805-927-9637
Spanish spoken
WEBSITE *www.burtondriveinn.com*

LOCATION	In the center of old Cambria, just off Main Street.
OPEN	All year

DESCRIPTION	A renovated 19th-century inn decorated with plush modern furniture.
NO. OF ROOMS	Ten large suites with private bathrooms.
RATES	Year-round rates are $85-150 for a single or double. There is no minimum stay. Ask about a cancellation policy.
CREDIT CARDS	American Express, Discover, MasterCard, Visa
BREAKFAST	Continental breakfast is served in the guestrooms.
AMENITIES	Copier and fax; free parking; microwave, refrigerator, toaster, coffee-maker, TVs in every suite; king-size beds.
RESTRICTIONS	No smoking, no pets

CAPTAIN'S COVE INN

6454 Moonstone Beach Drive, Cambria, CA 93428   805-927-8581
Bonnie Cameron, Innkeeper
WEBSITE *www.thegrid.net/captainscove*

OPEN	All year
NO. OF ROOMS	Five rooms with private bathrooms.
RATES	Year-round rates are $85-115 for a single or double.
CREDIT CARDS	American Express, Discover, MasterCard, Visa
BREAKFAST	Breakfast baskets are delivered to guestrooms.
AMENITIES	Refrigerator stocked with soft drinks and juices; fireplaces; turndown service with mints; microwave, refrigerator, coffee-maker in all rooms
RESTRICTIONS	No smoking, no pets
RATED	AAA 3 Diamonds

FOG CATCHER INN

6400 Moonstone Beach Drive, Cambria, CA 93428   805-927-1400
WEBSITE *www.moonstonemgmt.com*   800-425-4121

OPEN	All year
DESCRIPTION	A large two-story English-style inn with country decor, located just steps from the beach.
NO. OF ROOMS	Sixty rooms with private bathrooms.
RATES	Please inquire about current rates and cancellation information.

BREAKFAST	Breakfast is served buffet style.
AMENITIES	Pool; rooms have fireplaces, coffee-makers, refrigerators, honor bars, microwaves.

J. PATRICK HOUSE BED & BREAKFAST

2990 Burton Drive, Cambria, CA 93428   805-927-3812
Mel & Barbara Schwimmer, Innkeepers   800-341-5258
Spanish spoken   FAX 805-927-6759
EMAIL jph@jpatrickhouse.com   *WEBSITE www.jpatrickhouse.com*

LOCATION	Exit Highway 1 at Burton Drive in Cambria. From the north, turn left; from the south, turn right. The B&B is just above the old village of Cambria.
OPEN	All year
DESCRIPTION	A 1984 two-story log home and carriage house with charming country decor and antique furniture throughout, surrounded by tall pines and country gardens.
NO. OF ROOMS	Eight rooms with private bathrooms. Try the Clare Room in the main house.
RATES	Year-round rates are $135-180 for a single or double and $170-180 for a suite. There is a minimum stay during holidays, and cancellation requires seven days' notice with a $20 fee.
CREDIT CARDS	American Express, Discover, MasterCard, Visa
BREAKFAST	Full breakfast is served in the dining room and includes orange juice, coffee, assorted teas, and hot chocolate; a fresh fruit bowl with toppings of nonfat yogurt, fresh local raisins, and homemade granola; breads or muffins with spreads; and a hot entrée.
AMENITIES	Wine and soft drinks and hors d'oeuvres, "killer" chocolate-chip cookies and cold milk in the evening, wood-burning fireplaces, fresh flowers throughout, chocolates at your bedside, the singing of birds outside your window, rubber duckie and bubble bath.
RESTRICTIONS	No smoking, no pets, children are welcome in the Clare Room. Molly is the resident pooch, a mixed shepherd.
REVIEWED	*Frommer's, Weekends for Two in Southern California: 50 Romantic Getaways, Karen Brown's California: Charming Inns and Itineraries, Fodor's, Damron Accommodations, Recommended Country Inns, The Best Places to Kiss in Southern California*
MEMBER	California Association of Bed & Breakfast Inns, Professional Association of Innkeepers International
RATED	AAA 3 Diamonds, Mobil 2 Stars, Best Places to Kiss 2.5 Lips

OLALLIEBERRY INN

2476 Main Street, Cambria, CA 93428   805-927-3222
Peter & Carol Ann Irsfeld, Innkeepers   888-927-3222
EMAIL *olallieinn@olallieberry.com*   FAX 805-927-0202
WEBSITE *www.olallieberry.com*

LOCATION	From Highway 1, take the Main Street exit in Cambria.
OPEN	All year
DESCRIPTION	An 1873 two-story Greek revival Victorian inn furnished with antiques; listed on the State Historic Register.
NO. OF ROOMS	Nine rooms with private bathrooms. Try the Creekside Suite.
RATES	Weekends and July and August, rates are $100-185 for a single or double. Midweek rates (excluding July and August) are $90-175 for a single or double. There is a minimum stay on holiday weekends, and cancellation requires seven days' notice.
CREDIT CARDS	American Express, MasterCard, Visa
BREAKFAST	Full breakfast is served in the dining room and includes fresh juice, coffee, tea, cereal, yogurt, fresh-baked muffins or bread, and a hot entrée. Special meals are also available.
AMENITIES	Afternoon local wines and hors d'oeuvres; coffee, tea, and home-baked cookies all day.
RESTRICTIONS	No smoking, no pets. The inn is inappropriate for small children.
REVIEWED	*Frommer's, Fodor's*
MEMBER	Professional Association of Innkeepers International
RATED	AAA 3 Diamonds

PICKFORD HOUSE BED & BREAKFAST

2555 MacLeod Way, Cambria, CA 93428   805-927-8619
Anne Larsen, Innkeeper

LOCATION	Heading north on Highway 1, turn right on Main Street. Go 0.2 mile and turn left onto Eton, left again on Wood, and left once more onto MacLeod Way. Heading south on Highway 1, turn left on Burton, right on Patterson, left onto Wood, and right onto MacLeod.
OPEN	All year

DESCRIPTION	A 1983 two-story Victorian inn decorated with antique furnishings from the 1930s, including Victorian chandeliers and a bar transplanted from the Buffalo Hilton in New York. The house overlooks Rancho Santa Rosa and the Santa Lucia Mountains.
NO. OF ROOMS	Eight rooms with private bathrooms.
RATES	Year-round rates are $109-145 for a single or double. There is a minimum stay during holidays, weekends, and summer. Cancellation requires seven days' notice.
CREDIT CARDS	MasterCard, Visa
BREAKFAST	Full breakfast is served in the dining room and includes coffee, tea, fruit juice, Danish, Danish pancakes, crepes, and omelets.
AMENITIES	Clawfoot tubs, afternoon wine and fruit bread at the circa-1860 bar, fireplace.
RESTRICTIONS	No smoking, no pets, well-behaved children are welcome.
REVIEWED	*The Official Guide to American Historic Inns*
MEMBER	California Association of Bed & Breakfast Inns

PINE STONE BED & BREAKFAST

221 Weymouth Street, Cambria, CA 93428   *805-927-3494*

SAND PEBBLES INN

6252 Moonstone Beach Drive, Cambria, CA 93428   *805-927-5600*
          FAX 805-927-0393

SQUIBB HOUSE

4063 Burton Drive, Cambria, CA 93428   *805-927-9600*
Martha Gibson, Innkeeper   *FAX 805-927-9606*
WEBSITE www.cambria-online.com/thesquibbhouseandshopnextdoor/

DESCRIPTION	An 1877 Gothic Revival–Italianate home decorated with pine furniture and flea-market finds.
NO. OF ROOMS	Five rooms with private bathrooms

RATES	Year-round rates are $95-125 for a single or double.
CREDIT CARDS	MasterCard, Visa
BREAKFAST	Continental breakfast is served in the parlor or guestrooms and includes fresh fruit, pastries, breads, and muffins.
AMENITIES	Fireplace, afternoon refreshments.
RESTRICTIONS	No smoking, no pets, accommodations are not suitable for children.
MEMBER	Professional Association of Innkeepers International
KUDOS/COMMENTS	"The rooms were wonderful and very clean. The B&B is right in town, so the shopping is close at hand ... I would definitely recommend this establishment to anyone seeking a peaceful and serene get-a-way."

WHISPERING PINES

1605 London Lane, Cambria, CA 93428   *805-927-4613*
Jack Anderson, Innkeeper   *FAX 805-927-4616*
EMAIL *jacka@thegrid.net*   WEBSITE *www.thegrid.net/whisperingpines*

LOCATION	Take Highway 1 north into Cambria. At the first traffic light, turn left onto Ardath Drive. Drive 1 block to Green Street, turn left, and go to the end of the road. Turn right onto Gleason Street.
OPEN	All year
DESCRIPTION	A 1987 two-story contemporary lodge; a suite of four rooms with private outside entrances.
NO. OF ROOMS	One room with a private bathroom.
RATES	Year-round rate is $125 for a single or double. There is a minimum stay on weekends, and cancellation requires 72 hours' notice.
CREDIT CARDS	American Express, MasterCard, Visa
BREAKFAST	Full gourmet breakfast is served in the guestrooms and features a 10-item menu.
AMENITIES	Spa robes and towels, outside hot tub.
RESTRICTIONS	No smoking, no pets, children over 10 are welcome. Infants are also welcome.

WHITE WATER INN

6790 *Moonstone Beach Drive, Cambria, CA 93428*   805-927-1066
EMAIL *innkeeper@whitewaterinn.com*   800-995-1715
WEBSITE *www.whitewaterinn.com*

OPEN	All year
DESCRIPTION	An English country inn and minisuites.
NO. OF ROOMS	Seventeen rooms with private bathrooms.
RATES	Please inquire about current rates and cancellation information.
CREDIT CARDS	American Express, MasterCard, Visa
BREAKFAST	Continental breakfast is served in the dining room or guestrooms and includes home-baked muffins, breads, fresh fruit, coffee, tea, or hot chocolate.
AMENITIES	TV/VCRs, king- and queen-size beds, refrigerators, hair dryers, gas fireplaces, video library.
RESTRICTIONS	No smoking, no pets

WINDRUSH

6820 *Moonstone Beach Drive, Cambria, CA 93428*   805-927-8844
Trudy Penfold, Innkeeper
Some German spoken

OPEN	All year
DESCRIPTION	A weathered-redwood host home with contemporary oak furnishings and ocean views.
NO. OF ROOMS	Two rooms with private bathrooms.
RATES	Please inquire about current rates and cancellation information.
CREDIT CARDS	No
BREAKFAST	Continental breakfast is served in the breakfast room.
AMENITIES	TV, refrigerator, ocean views, spacious rooms, king-size bed.
RESTRICTIONS	No smoking, no pets, ask about children.

CARLSBAD

This beach resort is a center for commercial flower growing and is now part of Oceanside. Named after the famous European spa (Karlsbad), the Southern Cal version is the home of LegoLand and the largest single-day street fair in California, held the first Sunday of every month from May through November. Carlsbad is about 30 miles north of San Diego.

PELICAN COVE BED & BREAKFAST

320 Walnut Avenue, Carlsbad, CA 92008   760-434-5995
Kris & Nancy Nayudu, Innkeepers   888-735-2683
EMAIL *pelicancoveinn@sandcastleweb.com*   FAX 760-434-7649
WEBSITE *www.pelican-cove.com*

LOCATION	Take I-5 to the Carlsbad Village Drive exit, head toward the ocean, turn left onto Carlsbad Boulevard, and take another left onto Walnut Avenue.
OPEN	All year
DESCRIPTION	A 1985 three-story Cape Cod inn decorated with a mix of contemporary furnishings and antiques, located within walking distance of the beach and village.
NO. OF ROOMS	Eight rooms with private bathrooms. Try the La Jolla or Laguna Rooms.
RATES	Year-round rates are $90-180 for a single or double. There is a minimum stay over weekends, and cancellation requires seven days' notice.
CREDIT CARDS	American Express, MasterCard, Visa
BREAKFAST	Full breakfast is served and includes a hot main dish, lots of fruit, cereals, hot coffee and tea, and juice.
AMENITIES	One handicapped accessible room, all rooms have fireplaces, two rooms with spa tubs, beach chairs, beach towels.
RESTRICTIONS	No smoking, no pets. Jett is the resident Lab.
REVIEWED	*Fodor's, Frommer's, Weekends for Two in Southern California: 50 Romantic Getaways*
MEMBER	California Association of Bed & Breakfast Inns, Professional Association of Innkeepers International

CARMEL

(CARMEL-BY-THE-SEA & CARMEL VALLEY)

Carmel is everything it promises: a picture-perfect seaside village with a dreamlike atmosphere, no fast-food restaurants, parking meters, or high-rises. Within its four-square-block central area are nearly 100 galleries, endless shops and restaurants and, on a good day, maybe Clint Eastwood. The Carmel Bach Festival gets underway in July. Point Lobos State Reserve is famous for sea otters, sea lions, and brown pelicans. Carmel is just south of Monterey off Highway 1.

CARMEL GARDEN COURT INN

PO Box 6226, Carmel Valley, CA 93924   *408-624-6926*

CARMEL VALLEY LODGE

Carmel Valley Road at Ford Road,   *831-659-2261*
Carmel Valley, CA 93924   *800-641-4646*
Michael Cawdrey, General Manager   *FAX 831-659-4558*
French, Spanish, and Russian spoken
EMAIL *info@valleylodge.com*
WEBSITE *www.valleylodge.com*

LOCATION	From Highway 1 north or south, take the Carmel Valley exit, which is 1 mile south of Carmel-by-the-Sea. Follow Carmel Valley Road 11.5 miles to Ford Road. The inn is on the left.
OPEN	All year
DESCRIPTION	A 1967 country inn consisting of 12 clusters of buildings with country and Shaker decor, situated on 3 landscaped acres.
NO. OF ROOMS	Thirty-one rooms with private bathrooms.
RATES	May through October, rates are $109-139 for a single or double with a private bathroom, $169-189 for a suite, and $289 for a cottage. November through April, rates are $129-169 for a single or double with a private bathroom, $199-219 for a suite, and $299 for a cottage. There is a minimum stay on weekends, and cancellation requires seven days' notice.
CREDIT CARDS	American Express, MasterCard, Visa
BREAKFAST	Continental plus is served buffet style in the dining room with fresh-made pastries, fresh fruit, juices, French roast coffee, and other beverages.

AMENITIES	Weekly wine tastings and walking tour of five wine-tasting rooms, meeting facilities for up to 40 people in country lodge conference center with stone fireplace, heated 60-foot pool, sauna, spa; horseshoes, Ping-Pong, complimentary s'more makings in all the fireplace rooms, special doggy treats at check-in, doggy hitching posts.
RESTRICTIONS	None. There is a $10 per day charge for pets. Lucky is the resident lodge dog. "Lucky is our Director of Barketing."
MEMBER	California Lodging Industry Association
RATED	AAA 3 Diamonds

CARRIAGE HOUSE INN

Junipero between 7th and 8th, Carmel, CA 93921   831-625-2585
Cathy Lewis, Innkeeper   800-433-4732
EMAIL *concierge@innsbythesea.com*   FAX 831-624-0974
WEBSITE *www.innsbythesea.com*

LOCATION	Exit Highway 1 on Ocean Avenue, then turn left onto Junipero (the first cross street as you enter the business district). The inn is on the right.
OPEN	All year
DESCRIPTION	A 1975 two-story rustic, shingled inn with French country decor, situated in the heart of the village.
NO. OF ROOMS	Thirteen rooms with private bathrooms.

Carriage House Inn, Carmel

RATES	Year-round rates are $189-249 for a single or double and $249-315 for a suite. There is a two-night minimum stay on weekends, and cancellation requires 72 hours' notice.
CREDIT CARDS	American Express, Discover, MasterCard, Visa
BREAKFAST	Continental plus is served in the guestrooms and includes juices, bakery items, cereals, ham- and cheese-stuffed croissants, fresh fruit, and hot beverages.
AMENITIES	Wine and hors d'oeuvres before dinner; cappuccino bar and sherry after dinner; all rooms have safes, wood-burning fireplaces, king-size beds, hair dryers, cable TV with complimentary Showtime, refrigerators, coffee-makers, iron and ironing boards, honor bar; some rooms have Jacuzzi or whirlpool tubs.
RESTRICTIONS	No smoking, no pets
MEMBER	California Association of Bed & Breakfast Inns
RATED	AAA 4 Diamonds, Mobil 3 Stars

COBBLESTONE INN

PO Box 3185, Carmel, CA 93921   831-625-5222
WEBSITE www.foursisters.com

CRYSTAL TERRACE INN

24815 Carpenter Street, Carmel, CA 93921   831-624-6400
WEBSITE www.bbhost.com/elegantinns   800-600-4488
                                              FAX 831-624-5111

OPEN	All year
DESCRIPTION	A renovated 1927 inn and cottage.
RATES	Please inquire about current rates. There is a minimum stay during some weekends, and cancellation requires seven days' notice, 30 days during special events, with a minimum $10 fee.
CREDIT CARDS	American Express, Diners Club, Discover, MasterCard, Visa
BREAKFAST	Breakfast is served buffet style in the lobby.
AMENITIES	Evening refreshments; the cottage has an antique four-poster brass bed, Jacuzzi, gas fireplace, and TV/VCR; most rooms with queen- or king-size beds and TV; some with VCRs, wet bars, refrigerators, and microwaves; one room is handicapped accessible.
RESTRICTIONS	No smoking

Forest Lodge

Ocean Avenue & Torres Avenue, Carmel, CA 93923   831-624-7023

Green Lantern Inn

Casanova Street & 7th Avenue, Carmel, CA 93921   831-624-4392
EMAIL info@greenlantern.com

Happy Landing Inn

Monte Verde Street, Carmel, CA 93921   831-624-7917

Hidden Valley Inn

102 W Carmel Valley Road, Carmel Valley, CA 93924   831-659-5361
EMAIL concierge@countrygardeninns.com   800-367-3336
WEBSITE www.countrygardeninns.com

Holiday Guest House

Camino Real & 7th Avenue, Carmel, CA 93923   831-624-6267
          FAX 831-625-2945
WEBSITE www.travelguides.com/inns/full/CA/1903.html

Monte Verde Inn

Monte Verde and Ocean Avenue, Carmel, CA 93923   831-624-6046

San Antonio House

PO Box 6226   831-624-4334
San Antonio Avenue & Ocean Avenue,
Carmel, CA 93921

Sandpiper Inn at the Beach

2408 Bay View Avenue, Carmel, CA 93923   831-624-6433
                                                    800-633-6433

Sea View Inn

Camino Real & 11th Avenue, Carmel, CA 93923   831-624-8778
Marshall & Diane Hydorn, Innkeepers   FAX 831-625-5901
WEBSITE www.bbchannel.com/bbc/p213716.asp

OPEN	All year
DESCRIPTION	A large Victorian inn decorated with antiques and oriental rugs.
NO. OF ROOMS	Six rooms with private bathrooms and two rooms share a bathroom.
RATES	Please inquire about current rates and cancellation information.
CREDIT CARDS	American Express, MasterCard, Visa
BREAKFAST	Continental breakfast is served in the dining room and includes juice, fresh fruit, yogurt, cereal, muffins, toast, and bagels. Breakfast includes a hot dish on Sundays.
AMENITIES	Four-poster, canopy beds, tea and coffee in the afternoon, sherry in the evening, library, garden, sitting room.
RESTRICTIONS	No smoking, no pets, the inn is not suitable for children under 12.
MEMBER	Professional Association of Innkeepers International

STONEHOUSE INN

8th Avenue & Monte Verde, Carmel, CA 93921   831-624-4569
WEBSITE www.carmelstonehouse.com   800-748-6618

OPEN	All year
DESCRIPTION	A charming, historic 1906 country inn decorated with antiques, located only a short walk to the beach.
RATES	Please inquire about current rates and cancellation information.
CREDIT CARDS	American Express, MasterCard, Visa
BREAKFAST	Full breakfast is served in the dining room and includes juice, coffee, fruit, and a hot entrée such as cheese omelets, orange French toast, or banana-rice pancakes.
AMENITIES	Fresh flowers, robes, teddy bears, sitting room, bicycles.
RESTRICTIONS	No smoking, no pets, ask about children.

SUNDIAL LODGE

PO Box J, Carmel-by-the-Sea, CA 93921   831-624-8578
EMAIL sundial@netpipe.com   FAX 831-626-1018

LOCATION	In the center of Carmel-by-the-Sea, a short walk from the beach.
OPEN	All year
DESCRIPTION	A contemporary three-story lodge built around a courtyard, with French country decor and Victorian furnishings.
NO. OF ROOMS	Nineteen rooms with private bathrooms.
RATES	Please inquire about current rates and cancellation information.
CREDIT CARDS	American Express, MasterCard, Visa
BREAKFAST	Continental breakfast is served.
AMENITIES	Telephone; refrigerator; TV; afternoon tea, port, and sherry.
RESTRICTIONS	No smoking, no pets

Sunset House, Carmel

SUNSET HOUSE

1 South East Camino Real, Carmel, CA 93923   *831-624-4884*
Dennis & Camille, Innkeepers   *FAX 831-624-4884*
Spanish spoken
EMAIL *sunsetbb@redshift.com*
WEBSITE *www.sunset-carmel.com/*

LOCATION   From the center of town, go west (toward the beach) on Ocean
                      Avenue for three blocks. Turn left onto Camino Real.

OPEN	All year
DESCRIPTION	A 1960 two-story English cottage trimmed in brick, with English country decor and ocean views.
NO. OF ROOMS	Four rooms with private bathrooms.
RATES	Please inquire about current rates and cancellation information.
CREDIT CARDS	American Express, Diners Club, Discover, MasterCard, Visa
BREAKFAST	Continental plus is served in the guestrooms and includes fresh fruit, award-winning baked goods, granola, fresh-squeezed orange juice, coffee, tea, and cocoa.
AMENITIES	Fresh-cut flowers, wood-burning fireplaces, five types of hand-split firewood, ocean views, TVs, telephones, wine tastings and lectures.
RESTRICTIONS	No smoking inside. Maggie and Guenther are the resident pooches.
REVIEWED	*Dog Lover's Guide to Carmel, Pets Welcome*
MEMBER	California Association of Bed & Breakfast Inns
RATED	AAA 3 Diamonds

TALLY HO INN

Monte Verde Street at 6th Avenue, Carmel, CA 93921   831-624-2232
John Wilson, Innkeeper   800-652-2632
Spanish spoken   FAX 831-624-2661
EMAIL *info@tallyho-inn.com*   WEBSITE *www.tallyho-inn.com*

LOCATION	Take Highway 1 to Ocean Avenue exit and go 1 mile to Monte Verde Street. Turn right and go 1 block to 6th Avenue. The inn is on the left.
OPEN	All year
DESCRIPTION	A 1941 two-story Comstock adobe inn with traditional decor, originally the home of cartoonist Jimmy Hatlo.
NO. OF ROOMS	Fourteen rooms with private bathrooms.
RATES	Year-round rates are $105-225 for a single or double and $225 for a suite. There is a two-night minimum stay on weekends, and cancellation requires 72 hours' notice.
CREDIT CARDS	American Express, Diners Club, Discover, JCB, MasterCard, Visa
BREAKFAST	Continental plus includes homemade breads, croissants, muffins, Danish, granola, oatmeal, fruit plate, orange juice, assorted coffees and teas.
AMENITIES	Free newspaper, robes, Jacuzzi tubs, hair dryers, irons and ironing boards, brandy in the evening, fireplaces, spectacular ocean views.

RESTRICTIONS   No smoking, no pets
REVIEWED   *America's Wonderful Little Hotels & Inns, Fodor's, Country Inns*
                magazine

VAGABOND'S HOUSE INN

Dolores & 4th Avenue, Carmel, CA 93923   831-624-7738
Sally Goss, Innkeeper   800-262-1262
WEBSITE *www.innbook.com/vagabond.html*   FAX 831-626-1243

OPEN	All year
DESCRIPTION	A charming inn decorated with antiques and designer fabrics, shaded by an oak tree, and surrounded by gardens.
NO. OF ROOMS	Eleven rooms with private bathrooms.
RATES	Year-round rates are $85-165 for a single or double.
CREDIT CARDS	American Express, MasterCard, Visa
BREAKFAST	Continental breakfast is delivered to guestrooms.
AMENITIES	Complimentary local newspaper, fresh flowers, waterfall, flagstone courtyard.
RESTRICTIONS	Pets are welcome, no wheelchair accessibility, the inn is not suitable for children under 12.

WAYFARER INN

4th Avenue & Mission Street, Carmel, CA 93923   831-624-2711

CARPINTERIA

PRUFROCK'S GARDEN INN

600 Linden Avenue, Carpinteria, CA 93013   805-566-9696

CORONADO

On the Silver Strand Peninsula in San Diego Bay, Coronado is accessible by bridge or vintage ferry. Some of the most beautiful beaches in all of Southern California are found here. The US Naval Air Station, where the military first made the unlikely pairing of plane and boat, is set up at the north end of the strand. Down at the southern end, check out Silver Strand State Beach and the historic Hotel del Coronado, which offers high tea and public tennis courts. The Lamb's Players Theatre is host to Southern California's only year-round professional theater troupe.

CORONADO VICTORIAN HOUSE

1000 8th Street, Coronado, CA 92118   619-435-2200

CORONADO VILLAGE INN

1017 Park Place, Coronado, CA 92118   619-435-9318

GLORIETTA BAY INN

1630 Glorietta Boulevard, Coronado, CA 92118   619-435-3101
WEBSITE *www.gloriettabayinn.com*

LOCATION	On Coronado Island across the bay from San Diego.
OPEN	All year
DESCRIPTION	An expansive, elegant 1908 two-story Edwardian mansion with chandeliers, marble stairs, brass banisters, and intricate moldings. The mansion overlooks Glorietta Bay and was originally the home of sugar baron John Spreckles.
NO. OF ROOMS	Eleven rooms in the mansion with private bathrooms.
RATES	Please inquire about current rates and cancellation information.
CREDIT CARDS	American Express, MasterCard, Visa
BREAKFAST	Continental plus is served in the veranda, the music room, or on the patio.

AMENITIES	Heat and air conditioning, music room with baby grand player-piano, complete business center, many rooms with kitchenettes, balconies, patios, swimming pool, concierge services, library, afternoon refreshments, gourmet coffee and tea available all day, laundry facilities.
RESTRICTIONS	No smoking

CROWLEY LAKE

RAINBOW TARNS

505 Rainbow Tarns Road, Crowley Lake, CA 93546   760-935-4556

DULZURA

Twenty-five miles southeast of San Diego on scenic Highway 94, Dulzura sits on the western edge of Cleveland National Forest. The Mexican border town of Tecate is 15 miles to the south.

BROOKSIDE FARM BED & BREAKFAST INN

1373 Marron Valley Road, Dulzura, CA 91917   619-468-3043
Edd & Sally Guishard, Innkeepers   FAX 619-468-9145
Spanish spoken
WEBSITE www.virtualcities.com/ons/ca/c/cax27020.htm

LOCATION	From the Dulzura Café, go east on Highway 94 for 1.5 miles and turn right onto Marron Valley Road. The Farm is the first driveway on the left.
OPEN	All year
DESCRIPTION	A 1928 farmhouse and stone barn with a barrel roof, decorated with handmade quilts, antiques, and local artwork, located in the mountains by Dulzura Creek.
NO. OF ROOMS	Eight rooms with private bathrooms and two rooms share a bathroom.
RATES	Year-round rates are $85-120 for a double. There is a two-night minimum stay in some rooms, and cancellation requires seven days' notice.

CREDIT CARDS	MasterCard, Visa
BREAKFAST	Full country breakfast is served and includes fresh-baked rolls and breads, homemade jams and jellies, egg dishes, fruit, coffee, tea, and juices. Four-course dinners are available by prior arrangement.
AMENITIES	Wedding facilities, gourmet cooking classes on weekends, hot tub, piano, terraces, gardens, grape arbor, fresh flowers, coffee-maker, sitting area, mini-refrigerator, oversized and clawfoot tubs, canopy beds, day beds, massage or aromatherapy, badminton, horseshoes, library, two rooms are handicapped accessible.
RESTRICTIONS	Smoking permitted in designated areas, no pets, ask about children. Pigs, ducks, goats, chickens, parakeets, doves, quail, peacocks and pheasants call Brookside Farm home.

EL CAJON

AT YOUR LEISURE BED & BREAKFAST

525 South 3rd Street, El Cajon, CA 92019   619-444-3124

ENCINITAS

Known mostly for its poinsettias, Encinitas bills itself as the "Flower Capital of the World." The fields of rare and exotic flora at the Quail Botanical Gardens are a visual and olfactory feast. Check out Cardiff-by-the-Sea, a charming, peaceful little beach- and hillside community just two miles to the south. Kick around the beautiful beach at Fletcher Cove or at any of the four State Beaches located within a handful of miles of Encinitas. Explore San Elijo Lagoon, a resting place for migratory birds. Local landmarks of note include La Paloma Theater and the golden domes of the enlightening Self Realization Fellowship. Encinitas is between Oceanside and San Diego on Highway 1.

CARDIFF BY THE SEA LODGE

142 Chesterfield Drive, Cardiff-by-the-Sea, CA 92007   760-944-6474
Jeanette Statser, Innkeeper
Some Spanish spoken
WEBSITE *www.cardifflodge.com*

OPEN	All year

DESCRIPTION	A large Victorian cottage with natural wood shingles.
NO. OF ROOMS	Seventeen rooms with private bathrooms.
RATES	Please inquire about current rates and cancellation information.
CREDIT CARDS	American Express, MasterCard, Visa
BREAKFAST	Continental breakfast is served in the dining room or on the terrace and includes fresh fruit salad, a variety of rolls and doughnuts, coffee, tea, juice, and cereal.
AMENITIES	Some rooms handicapped accessible, ocean views, fireplaces, whirlpool tubs, wedding facilities, rooftop garden with panoramic views, Jacuzzi.
RESTRICTIONS	No smoking in the rooms, no pets

LEUCADIA INN BY THE SEA

960 North Highway 101, Encinitas, CA 92024   760-942-1668

SEABREEZE BED & BREAKFAST INN

121 North Vulcan Avenue, Encinitas, CA 92024   760-944-0318
Kirsten Richter, Innkeeper
EMAIL *sansa@home.com*
WEBSITE *www.seabreeze-inn.com*

LOCATION	Three blocks from Moonlight Beach.
OPEN	All year
DESCRIPTION	A contemporary two-story inn with comfortable furnishings, overlooking the ocean.
NO. OF ROOMS	Five rooms with private bathrooms.
RATES	Year-round rates are $75-150 for a double. There is a two-night minimum stay on weekends and holidays, and cancellation requires seven days' notice.
CREDIT CARDS	Discover, MasterCard, Visa
BREAKFAST	Continental breakfast is served in the dining room.
AMENITIES	Reunion and business meeting facilities, waterfall and koi pond, king- or queen-size beds, telephone, fireplace, TV/VCR, patio, Jacuzzi.
RESTRICTIONS	Smoking in designated areas, children are welcome.

ESCONDIDO

About 30 miles inland from San Diego via I-15, Escondido is an emerging wine center of distinction. Tours and tastings are plentiful, and there are numerous festivals that celebrate the offerings of the vine, including the May Wine Festival and the New Wine and International Food Festival in November. Jazz concerts are plentiful from April through October, and the International Film Festival in September is a big draw. Escondido is also the main gateway to Mount Palomar Observatory and its 200-inch Hale Telescope.

CASTLE CREEK INN

29850 Circle R Way, Escondido, CA 92026   619-751-8800
EMAIL sales@castlecreekin.com   800-253-5341
WEBSITE www.castlecreekinn.com

LOCATION	Thirty minutes north of San Diego.
OPEN	All year
DESCRIPTION	A luxurious inn situated in San Diego's wine country.
NO. OF ROOMS	Thirty suites with private bathrooms.
RATES	Please inquire about current rates and cancellation information.
CREDIT CARDS	American Express, Discover, MasterCard, Visa
BREAKFAST	Continental breakfast is served.
AMENITIES	Pool, hot tubs, tennis, wedding and meeting facilities, down comforters, private balconies.

ZOSA GARDENS BED & BREAKFAST

9381 West Lilac Road, Escondido, CA 92026   760-723-9093
Noli & Nena Zosa, Innkeepers   800-711-8361
Philippino and Spanish spoken   FAX 760-723-3460
EMAIL zosabnb@pacbell.net   *WEBSITE www.zosagardens.com*

LOCATION	From San Diego, head north on Highway 15 and exit onto Highway 395. Turn left onto Highway 395, go up the hill 1 mile, take a right on West Lilac Road, and drive 1.5 miles to Lilac Walk. Take a right, then a left through the big gates.
OPEN	All year except Christmas
DESCRIPTION	A 1942 Spanish hacienda and 1985 addition with contemporary furnishings, situated on a secluded plateau in wine country with 22 acres of gardens.

NO. OF ROOMS	Nine rooms with private bathrooms. The cottage has two bedrooms with a shared bath.
RATES	February through October, rates are $139-250 for a single or double, $165-225 for a suite, and $250 for the cottage. November through January, rates are $125-225 for a single or double, $155-200 for a suite, and $200 for the cottage. There is no minimum stay, and cancellation requires one week's notice with a $25 fee.
CREDIT CARDS	American Express, Diners Club, Discover, MasterCard, Visa
BREAKFAST	Full breakfast is served in the dining room or by the pool and includes fresh guava or orange juice from the orchards, homemade apple muffins, eggs Benedict with avocado picked from the trees, frittata, fresh fruit, and scones. Special dietary needs can be accommodated with advance notice.
AMENITIES	Fresh flowers in rooms, robes, video library, popcorn, cookies, brownies, hot chocolate, tea, filtered water, happy hour with wine and hors d'oeuvres, Jacuzzi, tennis court, horseshoes, volleyball, basketball, billiards, waterfalls, ponds, gazebos, willow swings in the courtyard, massage available at an additional charge.
RESTRICTIONS	No smoking, no pets. "This is really a place to get away from everything, including the kids. But they are welcome if well-behaved. The B&B is not a child-proof place." Sumo is the resident Akita, and there are five chickens and two quail on the property.
REVIEWED	*The Definitive California Bed & Breakfast Touring Guide, The Official Guide to American Historic Inns, Here Comes the Guide: Southern California*
MEMBER	California Lodging Industry Association
RATED	AAA 3 Diamonds, Mobil 3 Stars

FALLBROOK

Fallbrook lies about 20 scenic miles northeast of Oceanside and 50 miles northeast of San Diego off I-15. Golfers will thrill to know that there are over a dozen golf courses in the immediate vicinity.

FALLBROOK COUNTRY INN

1425 South Mission Road, Fallbrook, CA 92028   760-728-1114
WEBSITE www.fallbrookca.org/fbcoinn.htm

LOS WILLOWS INN

530 Stewart Canyon Road, Fallbrook, CA 92028   760-731-9400
Al & Cathie Ransom, Innkeepers   888-731-9400
Spanish spoken   *FAX 760-731-6767*
EMAIL *loswillows@thegrid.net*   WEBSITE *www.loswillows.com*

LOCATION	Conveniently located off I-15, 45 minutes from the San Diego airport
OPEN	All year
DESCRIPTION	A 1997 three-story contemporary inn with elegant, upscale decor, situated behind electric gates on 44 acres with a private lake, vineyard, and avocado grove.
RATES	Ask about current rates and cancellation information.
CREDIT CARDS	MasterCard, Visa
BREAKFAST	Full breakfast is served in the dining room or outside on the patio and includes fresh fruits, juices, baked breads, fresh-ground coffee, and a select entrée. Lunch and dinner are also available.
AMENITIES	Whirlpool tubs and private balconies with panoramic views, TV/VCRs, in-room telephones with voice mail, individual climate control, fitness room with sauna, steam and massage rooms, outdoor spa, robes, afternoon hors d'oeuvres and wine hour.
RESTRICTIONS	No smoking, no pets, no children. Babe is the resident yellow Lab; Biff is the parrot. "Biff whistles the Marine Corps hymn. Babe fetches the newspaper and brings it to the inn."
MEMBER	California Association of Bed & Breakfast Inns, Professional Association of Innkeepers International

FAWNSKIN

At the northwest end of Big Bear Lake in the San Bernardino National Forest, Fawnskin offers a full plate of winter and summer recreations. Nearby are two major ski resorts and a fully accessible lake for boating, fishing, and other water sports. Help the town celebrate Old Miner's Day in July.

THE INN AT FAWNSKIN

880 Canyon Road, Fawnskin, CA 92333   909-866-3200
Kathy & Todd Murphy, Innkeepers   888-329-6754
EMAIL *tmurphy@bigbear.net*   FAX 909-878-2249
WEBSITE *www.bajalife.com/fawnskin/index.htm*

The Inn at Fawnskin, Fawnskion

LOCATION	From the town of Big Bear Lake, take Big Bear Boulevard east to the Stanfield Cutoff, turn left, cross the bridge, and turn left again onto North Shore Drive. Travel 3.25 miles to Canyon Road and turn right.
OPEN	All year
DESCRIPTION	A 1978 two-story log inn decorated with country furnishings and antiques, situated on 1 forested acre.
NO. OF ROOMS	Two rooms with private bathrooms and two rooms share one bathroom.
RATES	Year-round rates are $87-175 for a single or double with a private bathroom and $62-100 for a single or double with a shared bathroom. There is no minimum stay, and cancellation requires 10 days' notice, 30 days during holidays.
CREDIT CARDS	American Express, MasterCard, Visa
BREAKFAST	Full gourmet breakfast is served in the dining room and includes beverages, an entrée, meat, and fruit.
AMENITIES	Terry robes; afternoon hors d'oeuvres; bottomless cookie jar; game room with pool table, wide-screen TV, video library, electronic darts, game table; a basket of books is available.
RESTRICTIONS	No smoking inside, children over six are welcome.
REVIEWED	*Romantic Southern California*
RATED	AAA 2 Diamonds

WINDY POINT INN BED & BREAKFAST

39015 North Shore Drive, Fawnskin, CA 92333   *909-866-2746*
Val & Kent Kessler, Innkeepers   *FAX 909-866-1593*
WEBSITE www.windypointinn.com

OPEN	All year
DESCRIPTION	A contemporary New England–style inn with eclectic furnishings and panoramic views of the lake.
NO. OF ROOMS	Five rooms with private bathrooms.
RATES	Year-round rates are $125-245 for a double. Ask about a cancellation policy.
CREDIT CARDS	American Express, Discover, MasterCard, Visa
BREAKFAST	Full breakfast is served and includes banana-stuffed cinnamon French toast, Spanish frittata, and side dishes such as potatoes and fresh fruit.
AMENITIES	Featherbeds, conversation pit, grand piano, stocked refrigerator, wood-burning fireplace, all rooms have views of the lake, four rooms have two-person whirlpools facing the lake, bubble bath, fresh flowers, homemade cookies on arrival, ice buckets and glasses, fully stocked wet bar, private boat dock.
RESTRICTIONS	No smoking, no pets, the inn is not suitable for children.
REVIEWED	*Sunset* magazine, *Weekends for Two in Southern California, The Best Places to Kiss in Southern California, Wonderful Weekends from LA, Frommer's*
MEMBER	Southern California Bed & Breakfast Association
KUDOS/COMMENTS	"Exquisite lake views, romantic getaway." "The decor was great and a wonderful gourmet breakfast was served on the patio beside the lake."

GOLETA

CIRCLE BAR B GUEST RANCH

1800 Refugio Road, Goleta, CA 93117   *805-968-1113*
EMAIL circleb@silcom.com   *WEBSITE www.circlebarb.com/*

HANFORD

IRWIN STREET INN

522 N Irwin Street, Hanford, CA 93230   *559-583-8000*

HEMET

East of Los Angeles and about 40 miles southwest of Palm Springs on scenic Highway 74, Hemet rests just north of the wonderful wine country of Temecula Valley. Tour the vineyards or drive a few miles west to San Bernardino National Forest and Mount San Jacinto State Park.

HEARTS HOME FARM BED & BREAKFAST

32643 Highway 74, Hemet, CA 92545   *909-926-3343*
Lawrence & Ana Shurtz, Innkeepers   *800-965-1606*
EMAIL heartshomefarm@yahoo.com   *FAX 909-926-8814*
WEBSITE www.heartshome.com

LOCATION	From Highway 215, take Highway 74 east for 6 miles.
OPEN	All year
DESCRIPTION	Restored early 1900s two-bedroom country cottages with 1930s decor and stucco, lattice, and plaster work, secluded in a ring of trees and flowering gardens, reminiscent of a quaint European setting.
NO. OF ROOMS	Two rooms with private bathrooms and two rooms share two bathrooms.
RATES	Year-round rates are $110-125 for a two-bedroom cottage. There is a minimum stay during Thanksgiving and Christmas, and cancellation requires seven days' notice.
CREDIT CARDS	MasterCard, Visa
BREAKFAST	Continental plus is supplied in the cottage kitchens and includes fresh breads, yogurt, cereals, fresh fruits, juice, coffee, teas. The tables are set and ready.
AMENITIES	Satellite TV, central air, fireplace, bottle of Temecula Valley wine.
RESTRICTIONS	No smoking, no pets. Jessy Jane is the resident pooch.

HOLLYWOOD

ANNA'S BED & BREAKFAST

10926 Hamlin Street, North Hollywood, CA 91606   818-980-6191

IDYLLWILD

An alpine resort town a mile high in the spectacular San Jacinto Mountains, east of Los Angeles and southeast of San Bernardino via I-10 and Highway 243. The performing arts are showcased here year-round at the Idyllwild School of Music and Arts with free performances every weekend, and the Idyllwild Jazz Festival in August is well worth your time. Other celebrations include the Strawberry Valley Festival in mid-May and the Idyllwild Film Festival in October.

CEDAR STREET INN

25870 Cedar Street, Idyllwild, CA 92549   909-659-4789

CREEKSTONE INN

54950 Pine Crest Avenue, Idyllwild, CA 92549   909-659-3342
Judith Smith, Innkeeper   800-409-2127
WEBSITE www.idyllwild.com

LOCATION	Less than a mile east of the village center. Turn left at the stop sign.
OPEN	All year
DESCRIPTION	A renovated 1942 two-story alpine inn with original wood paneling and creekstone construction.
NO. OF ROOMS	Nine rooms with private bathrooms.
RATES	Year-round rates are $95-145 for a single or double. There is a two-night minimum stay on weekends, three nights on holidays. Cancellation requires 14 days' notice.
CREDIT CARDS	MasterCard, Visa
BREAKFAST	Full breakfast is served in the dining room and includes juice, fruit, a hot entrée, coffee, and assorted teas.

Creekstone Inn, Idyllwild

AMENITIES	Handicapped accessible, seven rooms with fireplaces, three with double Jacuzzis, hot beverages available at all times, refrigerator for guest use, pool table, refreshments served Friday afternoons at 4 p.m., telephone in lobby.
RESTRICTIONS	No smoking inside, no children
MEMBER	Professional Association of Innkeepers International, California Lodging Industry Association
RATED	AAA 3 Diamonds
AWARDS	1996, One of the Best Places to Stay in California, *Los Angeles Times* reader's poll

FERN VALLEY INN

25240 Fern Valley Road, Idyllwild, CA 92549   909-659-2205
EMAIL fernvalleyinn@idyllwild.com
WEBSITE www.idyllwild.com/ferninn.htm

THE PINE COVE INN

23481 Highway 243, Idyllwild, CA 92549	909-659-5033
Bob & Michelle Bollmann, Innkeepers	888-659-5033
WEBSITE www.idyllwild.com	FAX 909-659-5034

LOCATION
Three miles north of the center of town on Highway 243, 1 hour from Palm Springs.

OPEN
All year

DESCRIPTION
A two-story mountain lodge and three two-story A-frame chalets with mountainesque decor.

NO. OF ROOMS
Ten rooms with private bathrooms.

RATES
Year-round rates are $70-100 for a single or double. Please inquire about cancellation information.

CREDIT CARDS
American Express, Discover, MasterCard, Visa

BREAKFAST
Full breakfast is served in the dining room or guestrooms and includes cereals, coffeecake or muffins, fresh-squeezed orange juice, fresh fruit, and a hot entrée such as French toast, pancakes, or omelets.

AMENITIES
TV/VCR lounge, conference room, lodge has a large fireplace, hammock.

RESTRICTIONS
No pets

REVIEWED
Inn Places, The Damron Guide

RATED
Mobil 1 Star

RAINBOW INN ON STRAWBERRY CREEK

54420 South Circle Drive, Idyllwild, CA 92549	909-659-0111
EMAIL rainbwinn@aol.com	WEBSITE www.idyllwild.com/rainbow.htm

OPEN
All year

DESCRIPTION
A two-story inn situated beside a creek high in the San Jacinto Mountains.

NO. OF ROOMS
Five bedrooms with private bathrooms.

RATES
Please inquire about current rates. There is a two-night minimum stay during weekends, three or four nights during major holidays.

BREAKFAST
Full breakfast is served.

AMENITIES	Wood-burning fireplace, gardens, two large decks, conference center; one room with a king-size bed and two-person Jacuzzi; three rooms with queen-size beds; three rooms with fireplaces.
RESTRICTIONS	No smoking, no pets

STRAWBERRY CREEK INN, INC.

26370 Highway 243, Idyllwild, CA 92549
Giana Dugan & Jim Goff, Innkeepers
WEBSITE *www.strawberrycreekinn.com*

909-659-3202
800-262-8969

OPEN	All year
DESCRIPTION	A country inn and separate cottage, located in a rural village in the San Jacinto Mountains, surrounded by hundreds of miles of hiking trails.
NO. OF ROOMS	Nine rooms with private bathrooms.
RATES	Year-round rates are $75-150 for a single or double. There is a two-night minimum stay on weekends and cancellation requires 14 days' notice.
CREDIT CARDS	Discover, MasterCard, Visa
BREAKFAST	Full breakfast is served in the dining room and includes specialties such as baked German French toast with smoked bratwurst or applesauce pancakes.
AMENITIES	Afternoon wine, library, fireplace, sitting room, refrigerators, queen-size beds, limited handicapped access.
RESTRICTIONS	No smoking, no pets, ask about children.

JOSHUA TREE

Fifteen miles west of Twentynine Palms on scenic Highway 62, Joshua Tree is a tiny high-desert town on the doorstep of half-a-million-acre Joshua Tree National Park. Bird-watchers, hikers, geology enthusiasts will all love it here. Visit Pioneertown and the Hi-Desert Playhouse.

JOSHUA TREE INN

61259 29 Palms Highway, Joshua Tree, CA 92252   760-366-1188
WEBSITE www.joshuatreeinn.com   800-366-1444
          FAX 760-366-3805

OPEN	All year
DESCRIPTION	A ranch-style hacienda with a red-tile roof, decorated with antiques, and situated in a beautiful desert setting.
NO. OF ROOMS	All rooms with private bathrooms.
RATES	Please inquire about current rates. Cancellation requires 72 hours' notice, seven days during holidays.
CREDIT CARDS	MasterCard, Visa
BREAKFAST	Full breakfast is available. Box lunches are prepared with advance notice.
AMENITIES	Pool, therapeutic massages available, fax, horse corrals.
RESTRICTIONS	Smoking is limited. Please ask about pets.

JULIAN

Dozens of orchards—peach, pear, and, in particular, apple—quilt the countryside around this historic gold-mining townsite. There are also three local wineries. Sample the fruits and wines, tour the historic buildings, visit the working gold mines, and don't miss the Julian Wolf Preserve. The wildflowers are gorgeous here in spring. Feast on Julian's famous apple pies during the annual Apple Day Celebration in October. From Escondido, 34 miles southeast via Highway 78.

THE ARTISTS' LOFT B&B AND
THE CABINS AT STRAWBERRY HILL

4811 Pine Ridge Avenue, Julian, CA 92036   760 765-0765
Chuck Kimball & Nanessence, Innkeepers
EMAIL mail@artistsloft.com
WEBSITE www.artistsloft.com

LOCATION	One mile west of Julian.
OPEN	All year
DESCRIPTION	A 1962 ranch home and two 1929 Craftsman-style cabins eclectically decorated with antiques, comfortable furnishings, and natural woods, situated on 10 acres of woods in the Cleveland National Forest with views to the Pacific Ocean.
NO. OF ROOMS	Four rooms with private bathrooms.
RATES	Year-round rates are $120-135 for a single or double and $145-165 for a cabin. There is a minimum stay on weekends and holidays, and cancellation requires seven days' notice.
CREDIT CARDS	MasterCard, Visa
BREAKFAST	Full breakfast is served in the Artists' Loft from a menu of more than 17 items, featuring everything from Russian to American to Indonesian dishes. In the cabins, breakfast is supplied for the first morning of your stay and includes eggs, juice, bread, and croissants.
AMENITIES	CD player with classical and New Age CDs, original art, lots of books, serenity of nature on 10 wooded acres; the Big Cat Cabin has a stone fireplace and the other rooms have antique wood-burning stoves; cabins have fully furnished kitchens.
RESTRICTIONS	No smoking. "Our facilities are fragrance free; please no perfumes or colognes."
REVIEWED	*The Best Places to Kiss in Southern California, Frommers' San Diego, Bed & Breakfast Southern California, Sunset* magazine
MEMBER	Julian Bed & Breakfast Guild (charter member)
RATED	Best Places to Kiss 3 Lips

EAGLENEST BED & BREAKFAST

2609 D Street, Julian, CA 92036   760-765-1252

EDEN CREEK ORCHARD GUEST HOUSE

1052 Julian Orchards Drive, Julian, CA 92036   760-765-2102

KUDOS/COMMENTS "Adorable furnishings. Great innkeepers, very fun people."

Historical House Lodging

2603 C Street, Julian, CA 92036   760-765-1931
WEBSITE www.historicalhouse.com

The Homestead Bed & Breakfast

4924 Highway 79, Julian, CA 92036   760-765-1536
WEBSITE www.homesteadbandb.com

LOCATION	About 3 miles from Lake Cuyamaca.
OPEN	All year
DESCRIPTION	A two-story host home decorated with antiques and heirlooms, with large windows looking out onto the hills of Julian.
NO. OF ROOMS	Four rooms with private bathrooms.
RATES	Please inquire about current rates and cancellation information.
CREDIT CARDS	MasterCard, Visa
BREAKFAST	Full gourmet breakfast is served in the dining room.
AMENITIES	Two-story rock fireplace, king-size beds, evening dessert, two rooms with fireplaces, one room with a clawfoot tub, space for small weddings.
RESTRICTIONS	No smoking inside
RATED	AAA 3 Diamonds

Horseman's Inn

3298 Old Cuyamaca Road, Julian, CA 92036   760-765-1034
                                                   FAX 760-765-1159

Julian Gold Rush Hotel, Julian

JULIAN GOLD RUSH HOTEL

2032 Main Street, Julian, CA 92036   760-765-0201
Steve & Gig Ballinger, Innkeepers   800-734-5854
EMAIL b&b@julianhotel.com   FAX 760-765-0327
WEBSITE www.julianhotel.com

LOCATION	In the center of historic Julian. From San Diego, take I-8 east for 35 miles and exit north on Highway 79. Drive 22 miles and turn left onto Main Street in Julian.
OPEN	All year
DESCRIPTION	A restored 1897 two-story Victorian hotel with American antiques. Listed on the National and State Historic Registers.
NO. OF ROOMS	Fifteen rooms with private bathrooms.
RATES	September through May, rates are $82-125 for a single or double and $135-175 for a suite or guesthouse. June through August, rates are $72-110 for a single or double and $125-160 for a suite or guesthouse. There is a minimum stay, and cancellation requires 48 hours' notice.
CREDIT CARDS	American Express, MasterCard, Visa
BREAKFAST	Full breakfast is served in the dining room and might include eggs Florentine, toasted date-nut-raisin bread, fresh fruit, queen's oats, orange juice, coffee, and tea.

AMENITIES	Hosted afternoon tea, meeting facilities for groups up to 25, free local calls, steps to shops and restaurants.
RESTRICTIONS	No smoking, no pets
REVIEWED	*Recommended Country Inns; Fodor's; Frommer's; The Best Places to Stay in California; America's Favorite Inns, B&Bs & Small Hotels; American Historic Inns: Bed & Breakfasts & Country Inns; The Complete Guide to Bed & Breakfasts, Inns and Guesthouses in the United States, Canada and Worldwide*
MEMBER	Professional Association of Innkeepers International, California Lodging Industry Association
RATED	AAA 2 Diamonds, Mobil 3 Stars
AWARDS	1993, Best of the West, *Sunset* magazine

JULIAN LODGE

2720 C Street, Julian, CA 92036   760-765-1420

JULIAN WHITE HOUSE

3014 Blue Jay Drive, Julian, CA 92036   760-765-1764
Alan & Mary Marvin, Innkeepers   800-948-4687
EMAIL *stay@julian-whitehouse-bnb.com*
WEBSITE *www.julian-whitehouse-bnb.com*

LOCATION	Sixty miles northeast of San Diego, 160 miles southeast of Los Angeles, and 4 miles from Julian's historic district. In Julian, go 1 mile south on Highway 78, turn left on Pine Hills Road, drive 2 miles, turn right on Blue Jay Drive, and go 0.5 mile.
OPEN	All year
DESCRIPTION	A 1979 two-story colonial-style plantation inn with Victorian decor and antiques, set back on a tree-lined country road.
NO. OF ROOMS	Five rooms with private bathrooms.
RATES	September through December, rates are $115-145 for a single or double and $160-175 for a suite. January through August, rates are $105-135 for a single or double and $150-165 for a suite. There is a minimum stay when a Saturday is involved, and cancellation requires seven days' notice.
CREDIT CARDS	MasterCard, Visa

BREAKFAST	Full breakfast, served in the dining room or guestrooms, is prepared from scratch and includes eggs Benedict, rosemary-roasted potatoes, and fresh-fruit crepes.
AMENITIES	Central air conditioning, robes in closets, spa in rose garden, afternoon sweets, king- and queen-size beds, rooms with fireplaces, whirlpool tub for two, antiques.
RESTRICTIONS	No smoking, no pets, children over 12 are welcome. Sissy is the resident cat. "Sissy is an outdoor cat, a 'working girl' in the country. She is friendly to our guests."
REVIEWED	*California's Best Bed & Breakfasts; Frommer's San Diego; Southern California: Off the Beaten Path; America's Favorite Inns, B&Bs & Small Hotels; The Best Places to Kiss in Southern California*
MEMBER	California Association of Bed & Breakfast Inns, Julian Bed & Breakfast Guild
RATED	AAA 3 Diamonds, Mobil 2 Stars
AWARDS	1997, runner-up, San Diego's Finest Service Award, San Diego Convention and Visitor's Bureau

LEELIN WIKIUP BED & BREAKFAST

1645 Whispering Pines Drive, Julian, CA 92036
Lee & Linda Stanley, Innkeepers
EMAIL *lodging@wikiupbnb.com*
WEBSITE *www.wikiupbnb.com*

760-765-1890
800-694-5487
FAX 760-765-1512

LOCATION	From the four-way intersection of Highway 78 and Main Street in Julian, go 1.5 miles east on Highway 78.
OPEN	All year
DESCRIPTION	A 1980 two-story cedar and brick home decorated with casual country decor, situated on 3 wooded acres.
NO. OF ROOMS	Four rooms with private bathrooms. Try the Willow Warren Room.
RATES	Year-round rates are $150-160 for a single or double. There is a minimum stay when a Saturday night is involved, and cancellation requires seven days' notice for a full refund.
CREDIT CARDS	American Express, MasterCard, Visa
BREAKFAST	Full breakfast is served in the dining room and includes fresh pastries, juices, fruit, an entrée, a side dish, and hot beverages.
AMENITIES	Flowers, robes, indoor and outdoor spa tubs, sparkling cider in rooms, afternoon dessert, satellite TV, llama treks, game room, library, 3 acres of grounds, fireplaces, private entrances.

RESTRICTIONS	Smoking is limited to outdoor areas, children over six are welcome. Three dogs, eight cats, two goats, one sheep, a miniature donkey, and 14 llamas roam the property.
REVIEWED	*Romantic Southern California, Romantic San Diego, Romantic Julian, Frommer's, Offbeat Overnights, Country Inns and Bed & Breakfasts*
MEMBER	California Lodging Industry Association, Julian Bed & Breakfast Guild

OAK HILL FARM BED & BREAKFAST

2333 Coleman Circle, Julian, CA 92036   760-765-2356

ORCHARD HILL COUNTRY INN

2502 Washington Street, Julian, CA 92036   760-765-1700
EMAIL *information@orchardhill.com*   WEBSITE *www.orchardhill.com*

OPEN	All year
DESCRIPTION	A two-story stone lodge with comfortable, elegant decor, perched on a hill overlooking Julian. The 4-acre, wooded property also includes four Craftsman cottages.
NO. OF ROOMS	Twenty-two rooms with private bathrooms.
RATES	Please inquire about current rates. There is a two-night minimum stay during weekends and holidays, and cancellation requires seven days' notice.
BREAKFAST	Full breakfast is served in the dining room or on the veranda and includes seasonal fruit, gourmet coffee and tea, and an entrée.
AMENITIES	Afternoon hors d'oeuvres; hammocks; reading benches; gardens; flower-lined pathways; all rooms have TV/VCR, Belgian chocolates, wine, fresh-baked cookies, queen- or king-size beds; the main lodge has a library and Great Room; cottages have fireplaces, porches and patios, wet bars, whirlpool tubs.
RESTRICTIONS	No smoking, no pets, no candles in rooms
REVIEWED	*Country Inns, Fodor's, Recommended Country Inns*
RATED	AAA 4 Diamond, Mobil 4 Star

PINE HILLS LODGE

2960 La Posada Way, Julian, CA 92036   760-765-1100
WEBSITE *www.pinehillslodge.com*

LOCATION	Three miles from downtown Julian.
OPEN	All year
DESCRIPTION	A restored 1912 rustic main lodge and cabins.
RATES	Please inquire about current rates and cancellation information.
BREAKFAST	Continental breakfast is served in the dining room. Lunch, Sunday champagne brunch, and dinner are served at the on-site restaurant.
AMENITIES	Dinner theater, large stone fireplace, pool.

RANDOM OAKS RANCH BED & BREAKFAST

3742 Pine Hills Road, Julian, CA 92036   760-765-1094

ROCKIN' A RANCH BED & BREAKFAST

1531 Orchard Lane, Julian, CA 92036   760-765-2820

ROCKING HORSE INN

5037 Highway 79, Julian, CA 92036   760-765-2429

SHADOW MOUNTAIN RANCH BED & BREAKFAST

2771 Frisius Road, Julian, CA 92036   760-765-0323
Jim & Loretta Ketcherside, Innkeepers   FAX 760-765-0323

LOCATION	From Highway 78 east, turn right 1 mile before Julian onto Pine Hills Road, drive 2 miles, and turn left onto Frisius Road.
OPEN	All year

DESCRIPTION	A two-story ranch-style inn with theme rooms, located among pine and oak trees on a mountainous, working ranch.
NO. OF ROOMS	Six rooms with private bathrooms.
RATES	Year-round rates are $100-130 for a single or double. There is a two-night minimum stay on weekends and holidays, and cancellation requires seven days' notice with a $10 fee.
CREDIT CARDS	No
BREAKFAST	Full ranch-style breakfast is served in the dining room and includes the guest's choice of juice, meat, eggs, cereal, rolls, and vegetables.
AMENITIES	Handicapped accessible, robes, hot tub, lap pool, meeting facilities for up to 17, outdoor games, pool table, catch-and-release pond, hiking trails, videos, TV, wood-burning stoves.
RESTRICTIONS	No smoking inside, no pets. Hanna is the resident pooch, Gaylanding is the quarter horse, and there are a number of cattle. "Calves are raised as project animals for 4H Future Farmers of America organizations."
REVIEWED	*The Best Places to Kiss in Southern California, You Are Cordially Invited to the Best Choices in San Diego, Offbeat Overnights*
MEMBER	Julian Bed & Breakfast Guild
RATED	AAA 4.5 Diamonds

KERNVILLE

KERN RIVER INN BED & BREAKFAST

119 Kern River Drive, Kernville, CA 93238   760-376-6750

NEILL HOUSE BED & BREAKFAST

100 Tobias Street, Kernville, CA 93238   760-376-2771

Kings Canyon

Montecito–Sequoia Lodge

8000 General's Highway, Kings Canyon, CA 93633

209-565-3388
800-227-9900

La Jolla

"The jewel" in Spanish, La Jolla is no misnomer. The sparkling, 7-mile Riviera-like coastline is the main attraction of this elegant, upscale playground, but La Jolla is also a noted research center that includes the Scripps Institute of Oceanography and the Salk Institute. La Jolla is minutes north of San Diego.

The Bed & Breakfast Inn at La Jolla

7753 Draper Avenue, La Jolla, CA 92037
Ron Shanks, Innkeeper
Spanish spoken
WEBSITE www.innlajolla.com/

619-456-2066
800-582-2466
FAX 619-456-1510

LOCATION   Take I-5 north from the airport to the La Jolla Village Drive exit, turn west to Tory Pines Road, and turn left. Drive to Ivanhoe, turn right, go to Silverado, and turn left. Go to Draper Avenue and turn right.

The Bed & Breakfast Inn at La Jolla, La Jolla

OPEN	All year
DESCRIPTION	A 1913 two-story cubist-style inn with elegant European decor. It was the home of the John Philip Sousa family in the 1920s and is listed on the State Historic Register.
NO. OF ROOMS	Fifteen rooms with private bathrooms.
RATES	May through August, rates are $149-249 for a single or double and $299-329 for a suite. September through April, rates are $109-279 for a single or double (weekend and holiday rates are $20 more). There is a minimum stay during weekends and holidays, and cancellation requires 10 days' notice with a $20 fee.
CREDIT CARDS	American Express, MasterCard, Visa
BREAKFAST	Full gourmet breakfast is served in the dining area, on the patio, or in the lush gardens.
AMENITIES	Afternoon receptions, fresh flowers, fruit and sherry in rooms, terry robes, complimentary minibars in most rooms, handicapped access limited to one room, air conditioning, fireplaces and ocean views in some rooms, cable TV in den, library.
RESTRICTIONS	No smoking, no pets, children over 12 are welcome.
REVIEWED	*Romantic California, The Best Places to Kiss in Southern California*
MEMBER	Professional Association of Innkeepers International, California Association of Bed & Breakfast Inns, California Lodging Industry Association, American Bed & Breakfast Association, San Diego Bed & Breakfast Association
RATED	AAA 3 Diamonds, ABBA 3 Crowns, Mobil 3 Stars

LITTLE LODGE OF LA JOLLA

2139 Torrey Pines Road, La Jolla, CA 92037   *619-551-3214*

SCRIPPS INN

555 Coast Boulevard South, La Jolla, CA 92037   *619-454-3391*

LA QUINTA

La Quinta is a remote little town on the southeastern edge of San Bernardino National Forest in the magnificent Coachella Valley. The surrounding desert landscapes and Santa Rosa Mountains are impressive. Explore Date Gardens and the Salton Sea, which sits at 235 feet below sea level. La Quinta is about 40 miles southeast of Palm Springs and 10 miles southwest of I-10.

TWO ANGELS INN

78120 Caleo Bay Drive, La Quinta, CA 92253   760-564-7332
Hap & Holly Harris, Innkeepers
EMAIL DeuxAnges@aol.com
WEBSITE www.bbonline.com/ca/twoangels

OPEN	All year
DESCRIPTION	A grand two-story French chateau, surrounded by landscaped gardens, bordering Lake La Quinta.
NO. OF ROOMS	Eleven rooms with private bathrooms.
RATES	Please inquire about current rates. There is a two-night minimum stay on weekends, holidays, and during desert events. Cancellation requires 14 days' notice.
CREDIT CARDS	American Express, MasterCard, Visa
BREAKFAST	Full breakfast is served in the dining room or on the terrace.
AMENITIES	King- or queen-size beds, gas fireplace, TV, phone, air conditioning, private patio or balcony, introductory yoga and meditation classes, wine and hors d'oeuvres in the evening, wedding and retreat facilities.
RESTRICTIONS	No smoking, no pets
REVIEWED	*Country Inns* magazine
RATED	AAA 4 Stars

LAGUNA BEACH

A beautiful and cozy seaside community, Laguna Beach is home to California's oldest art museum, gorgeous beaches, and the Laguna Playhouse. Summer festivals include the Art-A-Fair, Festival of the Arts, the Pageant of Masters, and the Sawdust Fine Art and Crafts Festival. Laguna Beach is just south of Newport Beach on scenic Highway 1.

CARRIAGE HOUSE

1322 Catalina, Laguna Beach, CA 92651   949-494-8945
Andy & Lesly Kettly, Innkeepers
French spoken
WEBSITE www.carriagehouse.com

LOCATION	Two blocks from the ocean, within walking distance of the galleries.
OPEN	All year
DESCRIPTION	A 1920s New England–style colonial beach house, the former home of Louis B. Mayer.
NO. OF ROOMS	Six suites with private bathrooms.
RATES	Please inquire about current rates and cancellation information.
CREDIT CARDS	MasterCard, Visa
BREAKFAST	Continental breakfast is served and includes granola, muesli, fresh fruit, tea, coffee, and juices.
AMENITIES	Four suites have kitchens; beach chairs and towels
RESTRICTIONS	Pet friendly, no smoking, central courtyard.

CASA LAGUNA BED & BREAKFAST

2510 S Coast Highway, Laguna Beach, CA 92651   949-494-2996
Kathleen Flint, Innkeeper   800-233-0449
Spanish spoken   FAX 714-494-5009
WEBSITE www.virtualcities.com/ons/ca/x/cax3501.htm

OPEN	All year
DESCRIPTION	A country inn and adjacent Cape Cod–style cottage furnished with antiques and collectibles, surrounded by tropical gardens and overlooking the ocean.

NO. OF ROOMS	Fifteen rooms with private bathrooms; four suites with kitchens and private bathrooms.
RATES	Please inquire about current rates and cancellation information.
BREAKFAST	Continental breakfast is served.
AMENITIES	Ocean views, wedding and meeting facilities, close to the beach, heated pool, panoramic views.
RESTRICTIONS	Smoking rooms available, pets and children are welcome.

LAKE ARROWHEAD

East of Los Angeles, high in the San Bernardino Mountains, this small and pretty year-round alpine retreat is a highlight of the scenic Rim of the World Drive. Skiing and water sports are the main events here. In the summer, tour the lake aboard the Arrowhead Queen for a view of the exclusive North Shore.

BRACKEN FERN MANOR

815 Arrowhead Villas Road, Lake Arrowhead, CA 92352   909-337-8557
Cheryl Weaver, Innkeeper   FAX 909-337-3323
Spanish spoken
EMAIL info@brackenfernmanor.com
WEBSITE www.brackenfernmanor.com

LOCATION	From Los Angeles, take Highway 10 east to Highway 215 north, then drive to Highway 30. Take the Waterman Avenue/Highway 18 exit, turn left, and take Highway 18 up the mountain 29 miles to Arrowhead Villas Road. Turn left and go two blocks.
OPEN	All year
DESCRIPTION	A 1929 three-story English Tudor country inn decorated with antiques and European furnishings.
NO. OF ROOMS	Nine rooms with private bathrooms. Try the Heather Suite.
RATES	Year-round rates are $80-115 for a single or double and $135-185 for a suite. There is a minimum stay during holidays, and cancellation requires three days' notice, seven days on holidays.
CREDIT CARDS	MasterCard, Visa
BREAKFAST	Full breakfast is served in the dining room or guestrooms and includes a different entrée each day, plus a meat, bran, fruit, cereal, juice, coffee, tea, and hot chocolate. Breakfast trays can be delivered to rooms if arranged at reservation time.

Bracken Fern Manor, Lake Arrowhead

AMENITIES	Game parlor with snooker, TV/VCR, classic movies; sauna; wine-tasting cellar; library; art gallery; garden Jacuzzi; chocolates; inspirational "pillow notes"; hammock; fireplace in the lobby; evening wine and hors d'oeuvres.
RESTRICTIONS	No smoking, children are welcome.
REVIEWED	*Frommer's, The Official Guide to American Historic Inns*
MEMBER	Professional Association of Innkeepers International
RATED	AAA 3 Diamonds

CARRIAGE HOUSE BED & BREAKFAST

---

472 Emerald Drive, Lake Arrowhead, CA 92352   *909-336-1400*
Lee & Johan Karstens, Innkeepers   *800-526-5070*
Dutch spoken
EMAIL *carriage_house@ramonamall.com*
WEBSITE *www.lakearrowhead.com/carriagehouse*

LOCATION	Follow Highway 18 from San Bernardino to Lake Arrowhead. At the signal, turn right onto State Highway 173 and drive to the second Emerald Drive.
OPEN	All year

DESCRIPTION	A New England–style country home with country decor, nestled in the mountains, with a view of Arrowhead Lake.
NO. OF ROOMS	Three rooms with private bathrooms.
RATES	Please inquire about current rates and cancellation information.
CREDIT CARDS	American Express, Discover, MasterCard, Visa
BREAKFAST	Full breakfast is served in the dining room and includes fresh-ground coffee, tea, fresh fruit and juices, pastries, Dutch babies, and a hot entrée.
AMENITIES	Afternoon wine and appetizers, sitting parlor, down comforters, TV/VCR, video library, woodland trails, hammocks, flagstone patio.
RESTRICTIONS	No smoking, no pets, not suitable for children under 12. Deke is the resident dog.

CHATEAU DU LAC BED & BREAKFAST INN

911 Hospital Road, Lake Arrowhead, CA 92352   *909-337-6488*
Oscar & Jody Wilson, Innkeepers   *800-601-8722*
Spanish spoken   *FAX 909-337-6746*
EMAIL *Chateau@js-net.com*   WEBSITE *www.lakearrowhead.com*

LOCATION	From the four-way stop sign at the entrance to Lake Arrowhead village, turn right and continue 3 miles to Hospital Road. Turn right to the first driveway on the right. Lake Arrowhead is located in the San Bernardino Mountains, 20 miles from the city of San Bernardino via Highway 18.
OPEN	All year
DESCRIPTION	A 1988 three-story contemporary/Victorian inn with French country decor, set on a bluff 200 yards above the shoreline.
NO. OF ROOMS	Five rooms with private bathrooms Try the Lake View Suite.
RATES	Year-round rates are $125-225 for a single or double. There is a minimum stay during summer and holiday weekends, and cancellation requires 72 hours' notice.
CREDIT CARDS	American Express, Diners Club, Discover, MasterCard, Visa
BREAKFAST	Full gourmet breakfast is served in the dining room and includes fresh fruit, coffee, tea, meats, and a rotating entrée such as an egg dish, sourdough/blueberry pancakes, chateau potatoes, or other special dishes.
AMENITIES	Afternoon tea, porch, gazebo. "The ambiance of a millionaire's mansion."

RESTRICTIONS	No smoking, no pets. Children are welcome; however, there are no special sleeping options beyond a queen-size bed in each room or suite. Maggie is the resident Maltese dog. "Our dog likes all people and is terribly spoiled."
REVIEWED	*The Best Places to Kiss in Southern California, Weekends for Two in Southern California, Country Inns* magazine
MEMBER	California Lodging Industry Association
RATED	AAA 3 Diamonds, Mobil 4 Stars

EAGLE'S LANDING BED & BREAKFAST

27406 Cedarwood Drive, Lake Arrowhead, CA 92352   909-336-2642
eagles_landing@southerncalonline.com
www.southerncalonline.com/eagles_landing.html

LOCATION	On the western shore of Lake Arrowhead in the San Bernardino Mountains.
OPEN	All year
DESCRIPTION	A large three-story mountain inn decorated with antiques, art, and mementos from world travels, with decks overlooking Lake Arrowhead.
NO. OF ROOMS	Three rooms and a suite with private bathrooms.
RATES	Please inquire about current rates and midweek discounts. There is a two-night minimum stay on weekends, three nights during holidays; cancellation requires seven days' notice, 14 days' during holidays and for multiroom reservations.
CREDIT CARDS	American Express, Discover, MasterCard, Visa
BREAKFAST	Full breakfast is made to order and served in the breakfast room. Brunch is served on Sundays.
AMENITIES	Evening refreshments; fireplace; suite has wood-burning fireplace, refrigerator, TV, covered balcony, and queen-size bed; guest lounge with library, TV/VCR, and large windows looking out onto the lake.
RESTRICTIONS	No smoking, no pets
REVIEWED	*The Best Places to Kiss in Southern California, Fodor's, America's Wonderful Little Hotels & Inns—West Coast*

GREYSTONE

831 Kuffel Canyon Road, Lake Arrowhead, CA 92352   909-337-9644
                                                    FAX 909-337-2169

LITTLE BEAR BED & BREAKFAST

191 South Highway 173, Lake Arrowhead, CA 92352   909-337-5470
WEBSITE www.mountaininfo.com   888-545-2327

OPEN	All year
DESCRIPTION	A restored 1940 two-story English Tudor inn.
NO. OF ROOMS	Two rooms, one suite, one cabin, all with private bathrooms.
RATES	Year-round weekend rates are $80-120 for a double. Please ask about a cancellation policy.
CREDIT CARDS	MasterCard, Visa
BREAKFAST	Full breakfast is served in the dining room, guestrooms, or on the patio and includes mushroom quiche, eggs Benedict, seafood crepes, muffins, scones, bagels, fresh fruit, granola, juice, tea, and coffee. A children's menu is available on request.
AMENITIES	Fireplace, grand piano, lake views; shampoo, lotion, and chocolates in rooms.
RESTRICTIONS	Smoking and pets permitted only in cabin, well-supervised children are welcome.

NORMANDY INN

247 Mittry Lane, Lake Arrowhead, CA 92352   909-867-3045

PROPHET'S PARADISE BED & BREAKFAST

26845 Modoc Lane, Lake Arrowhead, CA 92352   909-336-1969
KUDOS/COMMENTS "Beautiful, comfortable."

Romantique Lakeview Lodge

28051 Highway 189, Lake Arrowhead, CA 92352　　　909-337-6633
　　　　　　　　　　　　　　　　　　　　　　　　　800-358-5253

Lemon Cove

Lemon Cove is situated about 14 miles east of Visalia on Highway 198, the high road into the Giant Forest Village of Sequoia National Park. From here, you can access Kings Canyon National Park and enjoy good fishing at nearby Lake Kewah.

Mesa Verde Plantation Bed & Breakfast

33038 Sierra Highway 198, Lemon Cove, CA 93244　　559-597-2555
Scott & Marie Munger, Innkeepers　　　　　　　　　 800-240-1466
EMAIL relax@plantationbnb.com　　　　　　 FAX 559-599-2551
WEBSITE www.plantationbnb.com

LOCATION	Take Highway 99 to Visalia and head east on Highway 198 for 23.5 miles.
OPEN	All year
DESCRIPTION	A 1968 Southern plantation–style inn with rooms named after characters from *Gone with the Wind* and decorated accordingly.
NO. OF ROOMS	Six rooms with private bathrooms and two rooms share one bathroom. Try the Scarlett O'Hara Room.
RATES	Year-round rates are $99-159 for a single or double with a private bathroom and $69-89 for a single or double with a shared bathroom. There is no minimum stay, and cancellation requires seven days' notice.
CREDIT CARDS	American Express, Diners Club, Discover, MasterCard, Visa
BREAKFAST	Full breakfast is served in the dining room or on the brick courtyard and includes fresh-picked and squeezed orange juice; fresh fruit from the local fields; homemade granola; biscuits, muffins, and coffeecake made from scratch; and a hot entrée.
AMENITIES	Fresh flowers in rooms, robes, Jacuzzi in orange grove, heated pool, two gazebos, hammock, air conditioning, video library, murals painted by Marie on the inside and outside walls.
RESTRICTIONS	No smoking, no pets, children over 14 are welcome.

Mesa Verde Plantation Bed & Breakfast, Lemon Cove

MEMBER   Professional Association of Innkeepers International, California
          Association of Bed & Breakfast Inns, Sequoia Bed & Breakfast
          Association

LONG BEACH

Long Beach is centrally located and handy to all the vaunted sights and events of
the greater Los Angeles area. Don't miss the Queen Mary (docked just up the
road in Long Beach Harbor), the Aquarium of the Pacific, the Getty Museum,
Knott's Berry Farm, and the Historic Rancho los Alamitos. Seal Beach, a nice
little beach town, with an old-town main street and a large marina, lies just south
of Long Beach.

KENNEBEC CORNER BED & BREAKFAST

2305 E 2nd Street, Long Beach, CA 90803   562-439-2705
Michael & Marty Gunhus, Innkeepers   FAX 562-433-7776
EMAIL *kennebec@earthlink.net*   WEBSITE *bbhost.com/kennebeccorner*

LOCATION   Located 1.5 miles east of the Long Beach Convention Center, just
            2 blocks from the beach. Follow Ocean Boulevard east to the Long
            Beach Museum of Art (at the corner of Ocean and Kennebec), go
            north 2 blocks to 2nd Street and Kennebec.

OPEN	All year
DESCRIPTION	A 1912 two-story California Craftsman host home with comfortably elegant decor.
NO. OF ROOMS	One suite with a private bathroom.
RATES	Year-round rates are $95-140 for a single or double. There is no minimum stay, and cancellation requires seven days' notice.
CREDIT CARDS	American Express, MasterCard, Visa
BREAKFAST	Weekends, an elegant full breakfast is served in the dining room with silver, china, and candles. Early morning tea, coffee, and newspaper are delivered to the suite. Expanded continental is served on weekdays.
AMENITIES	Fresh flowers, robes, candlelit courtyard, cable TV/VCR, video library, bubble baths and bath oils, stereo with CD player, mini-refrigerator stocked with complimentary soft drinks, iron and ironing board, private telephone line and fax, courtyard spa, champagne upon arrival, sitting room with fireplace.
RESTRICTIONS	No pets, smoking permitted on the private balcony, children over 12 are welcome. Miki is the resident mutt; Kramer is the cockatiel; Fred is the fish. "All pets are really 'staff.' Miki will greet you and will never go into your suite, but loves to have you throw her ball while you're in the courtyard spa. Kramer will sing during breakfast and has hair like Kramer on Seinfeld. Fred the fish just swims."
MEMBER	*Southern California: Romantic Weekends; Bed & Breakfast—Southern California; The Official Guide to American Historic Inns*

LORD MAYOR'S INN

435 Cedar Avenue, Long Beach, CA 90802   *562-436-0324*
EMAIL *innkeepers@lordmayors.com*   *FAX 562-436-0324*
WEBSITE *www.lordmayors.com*

OPEN	All year
DESCRIPTION	A restored 1904 two-story host home with golden oak interior and period antiques. The home was built for the first mayor of Long Beach.
NO. OF ROOMS	Five rooms with private bathrooms.
RATES	Please inquire about current rates and cancellation information.
BREAKFAST	Full breakfast is served.
AMENITIES	Garden, sun deck, early morning coffee and tea.

Seal Beach Inn & Gardens

212 5th Street, Seal Beach, CA 90740
Marjorie Bettenhausen Schmaehl &
Harty Schmaehl, Innkeepers
German, Italian, Spanish, and Swedish spoken
EMAIL hideaway@sealbeachinn.com
WEBSITE www.sealbeachinn.com

562- 493-2416
FAX 562-799-0483

LOCATION	From I-405, exit onto Seal Beach Boulevard and turn left. Go approximately 3 miles to Pacific Coast Highway and turn right. Continue to 5th Street and turn left. The inn is on the left, at the second stop sign.
OPEN	All year
DESCRIPTION	An elegant two-story French Mediterranean–style inn decorated with comfortable furnishings and antiques, located one block from the beach.
NO. OF ROOMS	Twenty-three rooms with private bathrooms.
RATES	Year-round rates are $155 for a single or double and $195-325 for a suite. There is no minimum stay, and cancellation requires 72 hours' notice.
CREDIT CARDS	American Express, Diners Club, Discover, MasterCard, Visa
BREAKFAST	Full gourmet breakfast is served in the tea room and includes quiches, Belgian waffles, homemade granola, fresh fruits, and more.
AMENITIES	Evening tea and appetizers served fireside, fresh flowers in rooms, cozy robes, baskets with fruit and cookies, all rooms air conditioned, coffee and specialty teas available throughout the day.
RESTRICTIONS	Smoking in designated areas only. Children are discouraged.
REVIEWED	Elegant Small Hotels; The Complete Guide to Bed & Breakfasts, Inns and Guesthouses in the United States, Canada, and Worldwide; The National Trust Guide to Historic Bed & Breakfasts, Inns, and Small Hotels
MEMBER	International Innkeepers Association, California Historic Country Inns, American Bed & Breakfast Association, California Association of Bed & Breakfast Inns
RATED	ABBA 3 Crowns
AWARDS	1995, One of America's Top 12 Country Inns, Country Inns magazine; 1998, Mayor's Beautification Award, City of Seal Beach

The Turret House, Long Beach

THE TURRET HOUSE

556 Chestnut Avenue, Long Beach, CA 90802   562-983-9812
Nina & Lee Agee, Innkeepers   888-4TURRET
EMAIL *innkeepers@turrethouse.com*   FAX 562-437-4082
WEBSITE *www.turrethouse.com*

LOCATION	Travel south on the Long Beach (Highway 710) Freeway almost to the end of the freeway in downtown Long Beach; exit at 6th Street and travel 3 blocks. The inn is on the southeast corner of 6th Street and Chestnut Avenue.
OPEN	All year
DESCRIPTION	A 1906 two-story Queen Anne Victorian "painted lady" with period furniture, turrets, a wraparound porch, floral wallpaper, lace curtains, some antiques, comfortable overstuffed couches and chairs, beaded lamps, and wool floral carpets.
NO. OF ROOMS	Five rooms with private bathrooms. Try the Balcony Suite.
RATES	Year-round rates are $110-150 for a single or double. There is a minimum stay during special events and holidays, and cancellation requires seven days' notice, 30 days for special events.
CREDIT CARDS	American Express, Discover, MasterCard, Visa

BREAKFAST	Full gourmet breakfast is served in the formal dining room or in guestrooms upon request and may include juice, smoothies, or granita; seasonal fresh fruit (often baked or broiled); a hot entrée, breads, muffins, pop-overs; coffee or teas.
AMENITIES	Monogrammed robes, fresh flowers, afternoon tea and treats, after-dinner aperitif, concierge service, small meeting facilities, TV/VCR, stereo, air conditioning, fax, gift certificates, canopied beds, clawfoot tubs, scented gardens.
RESTRICTIONS	No smoking, children over eight are welcome.
REVIEWED	*The Official Guide to American Historic Inns*
MEMBER	Professional Association of Innkeepers International, California Association of Bed & Breakfast Inns
AWARDS	1996, Building a Better Long Beach, City of Long Beach, Department of Planning and Building; 1998, Landscapes for a Livable City, City of Long Beach, Department of Planning and Building

Los Alamos

In the heart of the flourishing Santa Ynez Valley, Los Alamos is about 15 miles south of Santa Maria on Highway 101, near Vandenberg Air Force Base. Close by, you will find old missions, wineries, and plenty of shops for antiquing. The Danish village of Solvang lies about 20 miles to the southwest.

1880 Union Hotel

362 Bell Street, Los Alamos, CA 93440   *805-344-2744*

LOCATION	Forty-five minutes north of Santa Barbara off Highway 101. Twelve minutes north of Solvang.
OPEN	Seasonal. The adjacent Victorian mansion is open all year.
DESCRIPTION	A restored 1880 two-story stagecoach-stop hotel decorated with antiques and Victorian period furnishings. Listed on the County Historic Register.
NO. OF ROOMS	All rooms share bathrooms.
RATES	Rates are $125-196 for a single or double. There is no minimum stay. Ask about a cancellation policy.
CREDIT CARDS	American Express, Discover, MasterCard, Visa
BREAKFAST	Full breakfast is served in the dining room and includes bacon, eggs, homemade blueberry muffins, fruit, hashbrowns or fried potatoes, orange juice, and coffee. Lunch and dinner are also available.

AMENITIES	Reflecting pool, garden, labyrinth, library, shuffleboard, collection of western and Victorian memorabilia, chess, checkers, antique pool table.
RESTRICTIONS	No smoking, no pets, no children. There are resident cats and a dog.
REVIEWED	*Le Guide du Routard*
MEMBER	Santa Barbara County Vintners Association

THE VICTORIAN MANSION

362 Bell Street, Los Alamos, CA 93440   805-344-2744

LOCATION	Forty-five minutes north of Santa Barbara off Highway 101. Twelve minutes north of Solvang.
OPEN	All year
DESCRIPTION	An 1864 three-story Queen Anne–Eastlake mansion with theme rooms.
NO. OF ROOMS	Six rooms with private bathrooms. Try the Egyptian Room.
RATES	Year-round rates are $198-250 for a single or double. There is no minimum stay. Ask about a cancellation policy.
CREDIT CARDS	American Express, Discover, MasterCard, Visa
BREAKFAST	Full breakfast is served in the dining room at the Union Hotel next door and includes bacon, eggs, homemade muffins, fruit, hashbrowns or fried potatoes, orange juice, and coffee.
AMENITIES	Bottle of champagne or local wine, lush robes, fruit and nuts, bubble bath, hot tub, fireplace, hidden bathrooms.
RESTRICTIONS	No smoking, no pets, no children. There are resident cats and a dog.
REVIEWED	*Le Guide du Routard, Offbeat Backroads, Country Inns* magazine
MEMBER	Santa Barbara County Vintners Association

LOS ANGELES

The West's largest city, a sprawling behemoth, actually does have a downtown area. Within and around its impressive and vital Civic Center are major art museums, the tri-theater Music Center for the Performing Arts, Natural History Museum, El Pueblo de los Angeles historical monument, and the international districts of Chinatown, Little Tokyo, and Olvera Street. Beaches, Hollywood, Disneyland, Beverly Hills, and more await exploration beyond the downtown area.

CHATEAU DU SUREAU

48688 Victoria Lane, Oakhurst, CA 93644   559-683-6860

THE COTTAGE

13 Toluca Estates Drive, Toluca Lake, CA 91602   818-762-7295
Sally & Nicolaus, Innkeepers   800-346-3040
German and some Spanish spoken
WEBSITE www.bestinns.net

OPEN	All year
DESCRIPTION	A charming two-story cottage surrounded by a garden.
NO. OF ROOMS	The cottage sleeps four to six and has two bathrooms.
RATES	Year-round rates are $95-110 for a double. There is a two-night minimum stay on weekends.
CREDIT CARDS	No
BREAKFAST	Continental plus is served.
AMENITIES	Pool, exercise equipment.
RESTRICTIONS	No smoking, no pets, ask about children
KUDOS/COMMENTS	"This was truly the best place we've ever stayed. The food was great, the Cottage was absolutely charming (I want to live here!), and Sally is a terrific hostess!"

COUNTRY INN AT CAMARILLO

1405 Del Norte Road, Camarillo, CA 93010   805-983-7171

ELAINE'S HOLLYWOOD BED & BREAKFAST

1616 North Sierra Bonita Avenue, Los Angeles, CA 90046   323-850-0766
Elaine & Avik Gilboa, Innkeepers   *FAX 323-851-6243*
French, German, Hebrew, Italian, Russian,
and Spanish spoken
EMAIL *Avikg@aol.com*

LOCATION	Go north on Hollywood Freeway to the Sunset Boulevard West exit and drive to the 7500 block of Sunset. Turn north on Sierra Bonita.
OPEN	September through June
DESCRIPTION	A 1998 two-story California bungalow.
NO. OF ROOMS	Two rooms with private bathrooms.
RATES	Year-round rates are $50-75 for a single or double. There is no minimum stay, and cancellation requires 24 hours' notice.
CREDIT CARDS	No
BREAKFAST	Continental breakfast is served in the kitchen or dining room and includes juice, tea, coffee, croissants, bagels, Danish, and fruit.
AMENITIES	TV/VCRs, videos, a tour of Hollywood.
RESTRICTIONS	No smoking. Kushi is the resident pooch; Crenshaw is the cat.

INN AT 657

657 West 23rd Street, Los Angeles, CA 90007   *213-741-2200*
WEBSITE *www.patsysinn657.com*

MULTIVIEW BED & BREAKFAST

3701 Multiview Drive, Los Angeles, CA 90068   *323-874-7302*

WHITE HORSE ESTATE BED & BREAKFAST INN

330 Las Lomas Road, Duarte, CA 91010   626-358-0798
Stephen & Christine Pittard, Innkeepers   888-774-9004
EMAIL *pasadena@travelbase.com*   FAX 626-793-6409
WEBSITE *www.citycent.com/whitehorse*

DESCRIPTION	A turn-of-the-century Queen Anne host home surrounded by large gardens, situated in the foothills of Rancho Duarte.
NO. OF ROOMS	Five rooms with private bathrooms.
RATES	Please inquire about current rates. Cancellation requires 72 hours' notice.
CREDIT CARDS	American Express, Discover, MasterCard, Visa
BREAKFAST	Full breakfast is served in the dining room.
AMENITIES	TV, air conditioning, telephone.
RESTRICTIONS	No smoking, no pets

THE WHITES' HOUSE

17122 Faysmith Avenue, Torrance, CA 90504   310-324-6164
Margaret White, Innkeeper

LOCATION	Five miles south of the airport.
OPEN	All year
DESCRIPTION	A contemporary host home decorated with eclectic furnishings and located in a quiet residential area.
NO. OF ROOMS	Two rooms with private bathrooms.
RATES	Please inquire about current rates and cancellation information.
CREDIT CARDS	No
BREAKFAST	Continental breakfast is served in the den.
AMENITIES	Antique piano, TV, telephone, one bedroom with a Pullman kitchen and private entrance.

LOS OLIVOS

WINE COUNTRY INN

2860 Grand Avenue, Los Olivos, CA 93441   805-688-7788
WEBSITE www.fessparker.com   800-446-2455

MALIBU

There is dramatic beauty in Malibu's thrilling, winding mountain canyons, and its beautiful beaches wash up surfers and the occasional celebrity as well. Don't miss Malibu Lagoon State Park, a haven for native and migratory birds, or the Getty Museum. Malibu is on Pacific Coast Highway, north of Santa Monica.

MALIBU BEACH INN

22878 Pacific Coast Highway, Malibu, CA 90265   310-456-6444
Spanish, French, and German spoken   800-4-MALIBU
EMAIL info@malibubeachinn.com   FAX 310-456-1499
WEBSITE www.malibubeachinn.com

LOCATION	Located in the heart of Malibu, next to the Malibu Pier.
OPEN	All year
DESCRIPTION	A 1989 three-story Spanish/Southwest–style hotel with Spanish decor. "Every room at the Malibu Beach Inn is designed to give you the feeling of being in your own private cottage on the beach."
NO. OF ROOMS	Forty-seven rooms with private bathrooms.
RATES	June through September, rates are $174-325 for a single or double. October through May, rates are $154-289 for a single or double. There is a two-night minimum stay on weekends and during holidays, and cancellation requires 72 hours' notice.
CREDIT CARDS	American Express, Diners Club, Mastercard, Visa
BREAKFAST	California continental plus is served on the terrace and includes a variety of fresh fruit, pastries, bagels, muffins, cereals, and juices.
AMENITIES	Private balconies with ocean views, in-room fireplaces, private Jacuzzi tubs, 24-hour room service, refreshment centers, TV/VCRs, robes, air conditioning/heat, in-room safes, handicapped accessible, meeting facilities.

RESTRICTIONS	No pets
REVIEWED	*The Best Places to Kiss in Southern California*, *Conde Nast Travel* magazine, *Travel & Leisure* magazine, *Vogue* magazine
RATED	AAA 3 Diamonds

MALIBU BELLA VISTA B&B

Malibu Canyon, CA   818-591-9353

MALIBU COUNTRY INN

6506 *Westward Beach Road, Malibu, CA 90265*   *310-457-9622*
EMAIL *info@malibucountryinn.com*   *800-FUN-N-SURF*
WEBSITE *malibucountryinn.com*   *FAX 310-457-1349*

OPEN	All year
DESCRIPTION	A restored 1943 Cape Cod–style inn with country decor, situated on the beach.
NO. OF ROOMS	Sixteen rooms with private bathrooms.
RATES	Please inquire about current rates and cancellation information.
BREAKFAST	Continental breakfast is served. The on-site restaurant serves lunch daily and dinner on weekends.
AMENITIES	Pool, telephones, cable TV, coffee-makers, refrigerators, two rooms with private Jacuzzis on patios overlooking the ocean, landscaped garden, suites have fireplaces and Jacuzzis.

MARINA DEL REY

Marina del Rey is the largest man-made boat harbor in the world. Soak up the yachty ambiance and sample the upscale goodies at the Cape Cod–like Fisherman's Village. Playa del Rey is a half-step to the south and Venice is a stone's throw to the north. The Getty Center is a must see, and Loyola Maramount University, just around the corner, offers cultural events throughout the year.

INN AT PLAYA DEL REY

435 Culver Boulevard, Playa Del Rey, CA 90293   *310-574-1920*
Susan Zolla, Innkeeper   *FAX 310-574-9920*
Spanish spoken
EMAIL *playainn@aol.com*
WEBSITE *www.innatplayadelrey.com*

LOCATION	From I-405, take the Marina Freeway exit (90 west) and go 2 miles to the stoplight at Culver Boulevard. Turn left and go 1.8 miles.
OPEN	All year
DESCRIPTION	A 1995 three-story Cape Cod–style inn with beach decor, located 3 blocks from the beach.
NO. OF ROOMS	Twenty-one rooms with private bathrooms.
RATES	Year-round rates are $145-295 for a single or double. There is no minimum stay, and cancellation requires 48 hours' notice.
CREDIT CARDS	American Express, MasterCard, Visa
BREAKFAST	Full breakfast is served in the dining room or guestrooms.

Inn at Playa del Rey, Playa del Rey

AMENITIES	Wine and hors d'oeuvres, tea and cookies, business center, garden hot tub, bicycles, beach towels, massages, facials can be arranged, all rooms handicapped accessible.
RESTRICTIONS	None. Children of all ages are welcome. "We have cribs, highchairs, and toys."
REVIEWED	*Karen Brown's California: Charming Inns & Itineraries, The Best Places to Kiss in Southern California, Weekends for Two in Southern California*
MEMBER	Professional Association of Innkeepers International, California Association of Bed & Breakfast Inns
RATED	AAA 3 Diamonds, Mobil 3 Stars

THE INN AT VENICE BEACH

327 Washington Boulevard, Marina Del Rey, CA 90291   *310-821-2557*
                                                         800-828-0688

MARINA BED & BREAKFAST

PO Box 11828, Marina Del Rey, CA 90295   *310-821-9862*
WEBSITE bestinns.net/usa/ca/marinabnb.html

LOCATION	Ten minutes from Los Angeles International Airport.
OPEN	All year
DESCRIPTION	A two-story contemporary host home with a rooftop deck.
NO. OF ROOMS	One suite with private bathroom.
RATES	Please inquire about current rates and cancellation information.
CREDIT CARDS	No
BREAKFAST	Continental breakfast is provided.
AMENITIES	Kitchen, rooftop deck, queen-size bed, TV, telephone.
RESTRICTIONS	No smoking, no pets, children over 12 are welcome.
MEMBER	Tourist House Association of America

MONTEREY

Monterey has it all: beautiful seascapes, enchanted forests of pine and gnarled cypress, and boundless options for recreation. The magnificent Monterey Bay Aquarium and historic Cannery Row and Fisherman's Wharf are tops on the to-do list. Within a handful of miles of Monterey, you will find three of California's most alluring towns: Carmel, Pacific Grove, and Pebble Beach. Festivals run year-round in Monterey. A painfully modest list includes Dixieland Monterey in March, the Monterey Wine Festival in April, the Great Monterey Squid Festival in May, the Monterey Blues Festival in June, Mozart in Monterey in August, the Monterey Jazz Festival in September, and La Posada and First Night Monterey during December.

DEL MONTE BEACH INN

1110 Del Monte Avenue, Monterey, CA 93940   831-649-4410

JABBERWOCK BED & BREAKFAST

598 Laine Street, Monterey, CA 93940   831-372-4777
888-428-7253

MERRITT HOUSE INN

386 Pacific Street, Monterey, CA 93940   831-646-9686
EMAIL info@merritthouseinn.com   800-541-5599
WEBSITE www.merritthouseinn.com

LOCATION	A five-minute walk from Fisherman's Wharf on Monterey Bay.
OPEN	All year
DESCRIPTION	An 1830 two-story adobe inn furnished with antiques, situated on a well-manicured property among magnolia, pepper, holly, and olive trees. The inn is listed on the National Historic Register and is part of the annual Monterey History and Art Association Adobe Tour.
NO. OF ROOMS	Twenty-two rooms and three suites with private bathrooms.
RATES	Please inquire about current rates. Cancellation requires 48 hours' notice.
CREDIT CARDS	American Express, Diners Club, Discover, MasterCard, Visa
BREAKFAST	Continental breakfast is served in the common room.

AMENITIES	Rose garden; all rooms have fireplaces, small refrigerators, telephones, and TVs; suites have separate parlors; some rooms with balconies; parking; innkeepers provide information, fix picnic lunches, and make reservations for area wine tours.
RESTRICTIONS	No pets
MEMBER	California Lodging Industry Association

MONTEREY HOTEL

406 Alvarado Street, Monterey, CA 93940   831-375-3184
WEBSITE *www.montereyhotel.com*   800-727-0960

LOCATION	In the heart of downtown Monterey, 1 block from the Conference Center.
OPEN	All year
DESCRIPTION	A restored 1904 Victorian hotel with plantation shutters, hand-carved furnishings, and a Hammond elevator with beveled glass.
NO. OF ROOMS	Forty-five rooms and suites with private bathrooms.
RATES	Please inquire about current rates and cancellation information.
CREDIT CARDS	American Express, Discover, MasterCard, Visa
BREAKFAST	Continental breakfast is served and includes fresh fruit, baked goods, coffee, tea, and juice.
AMENITIES	Afternoon refreshments in garden rooms; courtyard; fireplace; all rooms with marble baths and ceiling fans; master suites have tubs for two and sitting rooms; data ports, voice mail, conference facilities.

OLD MONTEREY INN

500 Martin Street, Monterey, CA 93940   831-375-8284
EMAIL *omi@oldmontereyinn.com*   800-350-2344
WEBSITE *www.oldmontereyinn.com*

OPEN	All year
DESCRIPTION	An elegant two-story inn with European decor, stained-glass windows, and skylights.
NO. OF ROOMS	All rooms with private bathrooms.
RATES	Please inquire about current rates and cancellation information.

BREAKFAST	Full breakfast is served.
AMENITIES	Concierge service; featherbeds; CD players; some rooms have wood-burning fireplaces; robes; bath salts and candles.
REVIEWED	*Bon Appetit, Country Inns, Romantic Hideaways*
RATED	AAA 4 Diamonds, Mobil 4 Star

MORRO BAY

The great 576-foot volcanic monolith that juts from Morro Bay is a protected nesting site for endangered peregrine falcons. Extending 4 miles toward this rock, the sandspit teems with sea life and is accessible to humans by shuttle boat. The truly physically fit will enjoy participating in the Morro Bay Triathlon in late September. The annual Harbor Boat Parade, held in early December, is a popular event. Morro Bay is a dozen miles northwest of San Luis Obispo on Highway 1.

MARINA STREET INN

305 Marina Street, Morro Bay, CA 93442   805-772-4016
EMAIL vfoster105@aol.com   888-683-9389
WEBSITE www.marinastreetinn.com   FAX 805-772-0667

OPEN	All year
DESCRIPTION	A two-story Victorian-style inn with theme rooms.
NO. OF ROOMS	Four suites with private bathrooms.
RATES	Please inquire about current rates and cancellation information.
BREAKFAST	Full gourmet breakfast is served.
AMENITIES	Afternoon wine and cheese, homemade cookies and milk in the late evening, fireplace.

VICTORIAN ROSE GARDEN BED & BREAKFAST

391 D Street, Cayucos, CA 93430   805-995-3382
Margaret Crofts, Innkeeper

OPEN	All year
DESCRIPTION	A restored 19th-century Victorian home.
NO. OF ROOMS	Three rooms, one with private bathroom.

RATES	Please inquire about current rates and cancellation information.
CREDIT CARDS	MasterCard, Visa
BREAKFAST	Full gourmet breakfast is served in the dining room. Vegetarian meals are available upon request.
AMENITIES	Fresh flowers, rose garden, down comforters, coffee delivered to guestrooms before breakfast.
RESTRICTIONS	No smoking, no pets, children are welcome.

NATIONAL CITY

DICKINSON—BOAL MANSION

1433 East 24th Street, National City, CA 91950   619-477-5363

NEWPORT BEACH

This melange of man-made islands is a bastion of Orange County's high society— a place where boats outnumber automobiles, and yacht clubs proliferate. The annual Flight of the Snowbirds Regatta in June is a major event. Check out the Baroque Music Festival in February and the Newport Beach International Film Festival in April. The Upper Newport Bay Ecological Reserve, southern California's largest estuary, is a vital stopover for migrating birds on the Pacific flyway. Newport Beach is on the Pacific Coast Highway, south of Long Beach.

BOAT & BREAKFAST

3400 Viaduct Oporto #103, Newport Beach, CA 92663   949-723-5552

DORYMAN'S OCEANFRONT INN

2102 West Oceanfront, Newport Beach, CA 92663   949-675-7300

The Little Inn on the Bay

617 Lido Park Drive, Newport Beach, CA 92663   714-673-8800
800-438-4466

Portofino Beach Hotel

2306 W Oceanfront Boulevard, Newport Beach, CA 92663   949-673-7030
Ken & Betty Ricamore, Innkeepers   FAX 949-723-4370
Spanish, Japanese, Russian, Armenian, Persian, and Turkish spoken
EMAIL *portofino@newportbeach.com*
WEBSITE *www.portofinobeachhotel.com*

LOCATION	Take Highway 55 to Newport Beach Boulevard and head south. Turn right onto 32nd Street, left onto Balboa, right onto 22nd Street, and then right onto Oceanfront Boulevard.
OPEN	All year
DESCRIPTION	A 1986 two-story European-style hotel furnished with antiques and Victorian decor.
NO. OF ROOMS	Twenty rooms with private bathrooms. Try the Portofino Room.
RATES	April through August, rates are $149-229 for a single or double and $279-339 for a suite. September through March, rates are $129-199 for a single or double and $259-299 for a suite. During weekends and holidays, higher rates are in effect for single-night accommodations. Cancellation requires 72 hours' notice.
CREDIT CARDS	American Express, Diners Club, Discover, Mastercard, Visa
BREAKFAST	Continental plus is served in the dining room and includes a variety of fresh fruit, home-baked biscuits and muffins, assorted cereals, yogurt, fresh orange juice, coffee, and tea.
AMENITIES	Each room has a private bath, TV, and private telephone; five rooms have Jacuzzi tubs; two premier rooms have magnificent panoramic views of the Pacific Ocean; some rooms have partial ocean views of the historic Newport Pier area; observation parlor with ocean views; surfing in front of the hotel; private guest parking; lounge with fireplace; fresh coffee and tea available at all times; complimentary newspaper.
RESTRICTIONS	No pets
REVIEWED	*Elegant Small Hotels; The Best Places to Kiss in Southern California*
MEMBER	California Lodging Industry Association
RATED	AAA 3 Diamonds

NIPOMO

KALEIDOSCOPE INN

130 East Dana Street, Nipomo, CA 93444   805-929-5444

OJAI

An idyllic Shangri-la, surrounded by national forest, Ojai is an artist's colony and a magnet for mystics. Soak in the spas at Matilija or Wheeler Hot Springs. Explore Lake Casitas, a treasure trove of coves and inlets. The Ojai Music Festival in June is a major event. Ojai lies at the edge of the Los Padres National Forest, 15 miles inland from Ventura via Highway 33.

CASA DE LA LUNA BED & BREAKFAST

710 S La Luna Avenue, Ojai, CA 93023   805-646-4528

DESCRIPTION	A Spanish-style hacienda.
NO. OF ROOMS	Seven rooms with private bathrooms.
RATES	Please inquire about current rates and cancellation information.
CREDIT CARDS	No
BREAKFAST	Full gourmet breakfast is served in the dining room.
RESTRICTIONS	No smoking, no pets

THE MOON'S NEST INN

210 East Matilija, Ojai, CA 93023   805-646-6635
Rich & Joan Assenberg, Innkeepers
WEBSITE *www.moonsnestinn.com*

LOCATION	In the heart of downtown Ojai, 1 block north of the center of town.
OPEN	All year
DESCRIPTION	A renovated 1874 two-story Arts and Crafts inn with eclectic furnishings, landscaped yard and gardens, a pond, and old oaks.
NO. OF ROOMS	Five rooms with private bathrooms and two rooms share one bathroom.

RATES	Year-round rates are $120-135 for a single or double with a private bathroom and $95-110 for a single or double with a shared bathroom. There is a minimum stay when a Saturday night is involved, and cancellation requires seven days' notice.
CREDIT CARDS	American Express, MasterCard, Visa
BREAKFAST	Full breakfast is served buffet style in the dining room and includes fresh fruit platter, assorted breakfast breads, granola, cereal, yogurt, coffee, tea, fresh orange juice, and a hot entrée served separately.
AMENITIES	Fresh flowers in all rooms; See's candies; bottled water; wine and light hors d'oeuvres; soft drinks, port, or sherry available in lobby.
RESTRICTIONS	No smoking, children over six are welcome. There are eight resident cats and two dogs.
REVIEWED	*Frommer's California 1999*

THEODORE WOOLSEY HOUSE

1484 E Ojai Avenue, Ojai, CA 93023   *805-646-9779*
Ana Cross, Innkeeper   *FAX 805-646-4414*
WEBSITE *www.theodorewoolseyhouse.com*

LOCATION	Drive 1 mile past the stoplight in Ojai.
OPEN	All year
DESCRIPTION	An 1887 two-story New England–style farmhouse of stone and clapboard construction with antique furnishings, wallpaper, and wainscoting, nestled onto 7 oak-shaded acres with views of the Topa Topa Mountains. Listed on the State and National Historic Registers.
NO. OF ROOMS	Six rooms with private bathrooms.
RATES	Year-round weekend rates are $95-150 for a single or double. Weekday rates vary. Please call for cancellation information.
CREDIT CARDS	No
BREAKFAST	Continental plus is served in the dining room.
AMENITIES	Air conditioning, swimming pool, hot tubs, croquet and volleyball courts, fireplaces, balconies, secluded setting.
RESTRICTIONS	No smoking, no pets. Oreo, Frenchie, and Kitty are the resident cats.
MEMBER	California Lodging Industry Association

OXNARD

CHANNEL ISLAND INN

Oxnard, CA   800-344-5998

PACIFIC GROVE

On the beautiful Monterey Peninsula, Pacific Grove was California's first state capitol. Today, along with neighbors Carmel, Monterey, and Pebble Peach, the area is a major tourist destination with much to do and see. Explore the rugged California coastline on the scenic 17-Mile Drive, and drop by the lighthouse at Point Pinos Reserve, built in 1885 and still operating. Don't miss the Monterey Bay Aquarium, Cannery Row, and Old Fisherman's Wharf. Monarch butterflies congregate here from October to March, hanging by the thousands in massive clusters that resemble dried leaves. The Monterey Jazz Festival is a major event, and there are numerous summer festivals.

CENTRELLA BED & BREAKFAST

612 Central Avenue, Pacific Grove, CA 93950   831-372-3372
Mark Arellano, Innkeeper   800-433-4732
EMAIL concierge@carmelinns.co   FAX 831-372-2036
WEBSITE www.centrellainn.com

LOCATION	Take Highway 68 west off Highway 1, which becomes Forest Avenue when you enter Pacific Grove. Cross Lighthouse Avenue, go 1 block to Central Avenue, turn left, and drive two blocks.
OPEN	All year
DESCRIPTION	An 1889 three-story Victorian inn with period decor, a cozy parlor area, and peaceful garden. There are also five cottages.
NO. OF ROOMS	Twenty-six rooms with private bathrooms. Try the Garden Room.
RATES	Year-round rates are $119-159 for a single or double, $159-209 for a suite, and $189-229 for a cottage. There is a two-night minimum stay on weekends, and cancellation requires 72 hours' notice.
CREDIT CARDS	American Express, Discover, MasterCard, Visa
BREAKFAST	Full breakfast is served in the dining room and includes waffles, egg dish, or biscuits and gravy, a choice of juices, fresh fruit, cereals, granola, yogurt, breads, muffins, or pastries.

Centrella Bed & Breakfast, Pacific Grove

AMENITIES	Wine and hors d'oeuvres each afternoon; coffee, tea, and cookies; one room with handicapped access; one room with Jacuzzi tub; garden.
RESTRICTIONS	No smoking, children are welcome in the cottages only.
MEMBER	California Association of Bed & Breakfast Inns

GATEHOUSE INN

225 Central Avenue, Pacific Grove, CA 93950   831-649-8436
Lewis Shaefer & Susan Kuslis, Innkeepers   800-753-1881
Spanish spoken   FAX 831-648-8044
EMAIL *lew@redshift.com*   WEBSITE *www.sueandlewinns.com*

LOCATION	Take Highway 1 to the Pacific Grove/Highway 68 exit. Follow straight (do not turn left with Highway 68) to Central Avenue and turn right. Drive 0.5 mile, turn right onto 2nd Avenue, and take the first left, into the driveway.
OPEN	All year
DESCRIPTION	A restored 1884 two-story Italianate Victorian inn decorated with period antiques and Bradbury wallpapers. Listed on the State and City Historic Registers.

Gatehouse Inn, Pacific Grove

NO. OF ROOMS	Nine rooms with private bathrooms. Susan recommends the Langford Room.
RATES	January through November and all weekends, rates are $110-165 for a single or double. December through May except holidays and weekends, rates are $75-125 for a single or double. There is a two-night minimum stay when a Saturday night is involved, and cancellation requires 72 hours' notice.
CREDIT CARDS	American Express, Discover, MasterCard, Visa
BREAKFAST	Full breakfast is served buffet style in the dining room, guestrooms, or garden and includes cut fruit, juices, hot beverages, home-baked goods, bagels, English muffins, cereals, and a sweet or savory main course that changes daily.
AMENITIES	Wine and hors d'oeuvres, never-ending cookie jar, soft drinks, turndown service with chocolates on pillows, special-occasion greetings.
RESTRICTIONS	No smoking, no pets, children over eight are welcome.
REVIEWED	*The Best Places to Kiss in Southern California, Frommer's, Fodor's, Inns & Outs*

MEMBER	California Association of Bed & Breakfast Inns, Professional Association of Innkeepers International
RATED	AAA 3 Diamonds, Mobil 3 Stars
AWARDS	1991, First Prize in Design Style, *Monterey Bay* magazine

GOSBY HOUSE INN

643 *Lighthouse Avenue, Pacific Grove, CA 93950*   831-375-1287
WEBSITE *www.foursisters.com*

GRAND VIEW INN

555 *Ocean View Boulevard, Pacific Grove, CA 93950*   831-372-4341

GREEN GABLES INN

104 *5th Street, Pacific Grove, CA 93950*   831-375-2095
WEBSITE *www.foursisters.com*

INN AT 213 SEVENTEEN MILE DRIVE

213 *Seventeen Mile Drive, Pacific Grove, CA 93950*   831-642-9514
Tony & Glynis Greening, Innkeepers   FAX 831-642-9546
Spanish, Thai, and French spoken
EMAIL *inat213@innat213-17miledr.com*
WEBSITE *www.innat213-17miledr.com*

LOCATION	From Highway 1 between Monterey and Carmel, take Highway 68 west. After the light at David Avenue, move into the left lane and continue on Highway 68 past the four-way stop sign. At the second stop, turn right onto Seventeen Mile Drive. The inn is 0.5 mile down on the right at Lighthouse Avenue.
OPEN	All year

DESCRIPTION	A 1923 two-story redwood Craftsman, a cottage that is surrounded by roses, and a third building with an interior and exterior of redwood. The decor is art noveau with leaded glass doors and rich wall paneling of oak, fir, and redwood.
NO. OF ROOMS	Fourteen rooms with private bathrooms. Try the Blue Heron Room.
RATES	May through October, rates are $135-240 for a single or double. November through April, rates are $100-200 for a single or double. There is a minimum stay on weekends, and cancellation requires 72 hours' notice.
CREDIT CARDS	American Express, MasterCard, Visa
BREAKFAST	Full breakfast is served in the dining room and includes a hot egg dish (eggs Florentine or Benedict), French toast prepared using thick cinnamon bread, pastries and fresh breads, orange juice, yogurt, cereal, and fresh fruit.
AMENITIES	Fresh flowers; robes; hot tub among the giant oaks; wine and hors d'oeuvres; beautiful lawn surrounded by flowers for small weddings; room for small group meetings; room with handicapped access; welcome basket with fresh cookies, mints, and bottled water; tea, coffee, and cookies available at all times.
RESTRICTIONS	No smoking, no pets, children over 12 are welcome.
MEMBER	California Association of Bed & Breakfast Inns, Professional Association of Innkeepers International

MARTINE BED & BREAKFAST INN

255 Ocean View Boulevard, Pacific Grove, CA 93950   831-373-3388
WEBSITE www.martineinn.com   800-852-5588

LOCATION	Four blocks from the Monterey Bay Aquarium.
OPEN	All year
NO. OF ROOMS	Twenty-one rooms with private bathrooms.
RATES	Please inquire about current rates. Cancellation requires 72 hours' notice.
BREAKFAST	Full breakfast is served on china with Sheffield silver and crystal.
AMENITIES	Complimentary newspaper; some rooms have wood-burning fireplaces; some rooms have ocean views; library; courtyard; game room with pool table; spa; baby grand piano; clawfoot tubs; off-street parking.
RESTRICTIONS	Smoking in rooms with fireplaces, no pets
REVIEWED	Country Inns, Bon Appetit

Old St. Angela Inn, Pacific Grove

OLD ST. ANGELA INN

321 Central Avenue, Pacific Grove, CA 93950   831-372-3246
Lewis Shaefer & Susan Kuslis, Innkeepers   800-748-6306
Spanish spoken   FAX 831-372-8560
EMAIL lew@redshift.com   WEBSITE www.sueandlewinns.com

LOCATION	Take the Pacific Grove/Highway 68 exit off Highway 1, then go straight onto Forest Avenue when Highway 68 turns left. Turn right onto Central Avenue, drive 0.5 mile, and turn right onto 7th Avenue.
OPEN	All year
DESCRIPTION	A 1910 two-story Craftsman inn decorated with French country decor and period antiques, with views of Monterey Bay.
NO. OF ROOMS	Nine rooms with private bathrooms.
RATES	June through November and all weekends, rates are $110-195 for a single or double. December through May, excluding holidays and weekends, rates are $75-125 for a single or double. There is a two-night minimum stay when a Saturday night is involved, and cancellation requires 72 hours' notice.

CREDIT CARDS	Discover, MasterCard, Visa
BREAKFAST	Full breakfast is served in the dining room, garden, or solarium and includes fruit salad, fruit juices, hot beverages, home-baked goods, breads and bagels, cereals, and a hearty main course served with savory egg dishes alternating with sweeter fare.
AMENITIES	Wine and hors d'oeuvres; snacks such as fruit, popcorn, soft drinks, cookies; flowers and robes; garden hot tub; special occasion greetings; romance packages.
RESTRICTIONS	No smoking, no pets, infants and children over five are welcome. Ashley is the resident pooch; Sequel is the Maine coon cat. "Ashley is small and mellow, very gentle. Sequel is seen in the garden but not heard."
REVIEWED	*Inns & Outs, The Official Guide to American Historic Inns*
MEMBER	California Association of Bed & Breakfast Inns, Professional Association of Innkeepers International
RATED	AAA 3 Diamonds

PACIFIC GARDENS INN

701 Asilomar Boulevard, Pacific Grove, CA 93950   831-646-9414
EMAIL *innkeeper@pacificgardensinn.com*   800-262-1566
WEBSITE *www.pacificgardensinn.com*   FAX 831-647-0555

OPEN	All year
DESCRIPTION	A two-story inn with Oregon pine furnishings and country decor, surrounded by cypress, oak, and pine trees.
NO. OF ROOMS	Twenty-eight rooms with private bathrooms.
RATES	Please inquire about current rates and midweek discounts. There is a two-night minimum stay on weekends, and cancellation requires 48 hours' notice.
CREDIT CARDS	American Express, MasterCard, Visa
BREAKFAST	Continental breakfast is served and includes fresh-baked breads, muffins, and sweet rolls.
AMENITIES	Evening wine and cheese; two hot tubs; all rooms have coffee-makers, telephones, refrigerators, cable TV; most rooms have wood-burning fireplaces; the two-bedroom suites have a full kitchen and living room; two rooms are handicapped accessible; free parking; conference center.
RESTRICTIONS	Nonsmoking rooms available
RATED	AAA 3 Diamonds

PACIFIC GROVE INN

581 Pine Avenue, Pacific Grove, CA 93950   831-375-2825

SEVEN GABLES INN

555 Ocean View Boulevard, Pacific Grove, CA 93950   831-372-4341
Ed & Susan Flatley, Innkeepers
French and Spanish spoken

OPEN	All year
DESCRIPTION	A three-story Victorian mansion with a grand Victorian parlor, decorated with antiques, located at the edge of Monterey Bay.
NO. OF ROOMS	Fourteen rooms with private bathrooms.
RATES	Year-round rates are $155-350 for a single or double. Call for cancellation information.
CREDIT CARDS	MasterCard, Visa
BREAKFAST	Full breakfast is served in the dining room and includes a hot egg dish, fresh fruit, rolls, pastries, and sometimes fresh fruit cobbler. High tea is also available.
RESTRICTIONS	No smoking, no pets, ask about children.

PALM DESERT

At the junction of Highway 86 and scenic Highway 74, Palm Desert delivers magnificent desert landscapes. Enjoy the boutiques, galleries, and restaurants of El Paseo, and discover why this strip is billed as "the Rodeo Drive of the Desert." The McCallum Theater for the Performing Arts and the Living Desert are both close at hand, and Palm Springs is a quick 20 minutes to the northwest.

TRES PALMAS BED & BREAKFAST

73135 Tumbleweed Lane, Palm Desert, CA 92260   760-773-9858
Karen & Terry Bennet, Innkeepers   800-770-9858
                                          FAX 760-776-9159

WEBSITE www.virtualcities.com/~virtual/ons/ca/d/cad3501.htm or
http://innformation.com/ca/trespalmas

LOCATION	Three blocks from the Palm Desert town center.
OPEN	All year
DESCRIPTION	A contemporary Mediterranean-style home surrounded by palm trees.
NO. OF ROOMS	Four rooms with private bathrooms.
RATES	Year-round rates are $80-100 for a single or double. There is a two-night minimum stay on some weekends, and cancellation requires seven days' notice.
CREDIT CARDS	American Express, MasterCard, Visa
BREAKFAST	Continental breakfast is served buffet style in the dining room or by the pool and includes fresh-baked muffins and breads, coffees and teas, fresh fruits, yogurt, and granola.
AMENITIES	Air conditioning, TV, king- and queen-size beds, pool.
RESTRICTIONS	No smoking, no pets, the inn is not suitable for children under 10.

PALM SPRINGS

The clean, clear air of this desert oasis, a former Cahuilla Indian village, began drawing the health conscious a century ago. Today's crowd tends more toward the rich and famous, but all can enjoy Palm Springs' near-eternal sunshine—350-plus days yearly. Take in the magnificent desert and mountain scenery from the valley or take the Aerial Tramway to the top of 8,000-foot Mount San Jacinto State Park. The Living Desert Reserve is a must see. The 70-odd, sun-baked golf courses here are fed daily by a million gallons of recycled water. Palm Springs is just west of Joshua Tree National Park, about 2 hours southeast of Los Angeles via I-10 and Highway 111.

THE 550

550 *Warm Sands Drive, Palm Springs, CA 92264*   760-320-7144
WEBSITE *www.the550.com/*   800-669-0550

ALPINE GARDENS HOTEL

1586 *E Palm Canyon Drive, Palm Springs, CA 92264*   760-323-2231
Tom Elefson & Bill Mattila, Innkeepers   888-299-7455

Spanish spoken
EMAIL hotel@alpinegardens.com

FAX 760-318-0155
WEBSITE www.alpinegardens.com

OPEN	All year
DESCRIPTION	A cozy single-level hotel surrounded by gardens, with most rooms facing the pool.
NO. OF ROOMS	Ten rooms with private bathrooms.
RATES	Please inquire about current rates and cancellation information.
CREDIT CARDS	American Express, Discover, MasterCard, Visa
BREAKFAST	Continental breakfast is served and includes fruit, muffins, rolls, Starbucks coffee, and juice.
AMENITIES	Outdoor pool, daily treats, hot tub, TV, air conditioning, phone, amenities basket.
RESTRICTIONS	No smoking

BACCHANAL—FOR MEN, IN THE HEART OF WARM SPRINGS

589 Grenfall, Palm Springs, CA 92264
Richard Anderson & Craig Novak, Innkeepers
WEBSITE www.bacchanal.net

760-323-0760
800-806-9059
FAX 760-416-4107

LOCATION	From Palm Canyon, head east on Ramon for 0.4 mile to Grenfall Road. Take a right and drive to the corner.
OPEN	All year
DESCRIPTION	A renovated 1954 single-story hotel with luxury suites surrounding a pool with mountain views.
NO. OF ROOMS	Eight rooms with private bathrooms.
RATES	October through June, rates are $79-129 for a single or double. July through September, rates are $69-109 for a single or double. There is a minimum stay during weekends, and cancellation requires one week's notice.
CREDIT CARDS	American Express, MasterCard, Visa
BREAKFAST	Continental breakfast is served.
AMENITIES	Heated pool, nine-person spa, video library.
RESTRICTIONS	No smoking, no children, all men.
REVIEWED	*Damron Guide, Spartacus, Out and About*

CASA CODY BED & BREAKFAST INN

175 South Cahuilla Road, Palm Springs, CA 92262   760-320-9346
Therese Hayes & Frank Tysen, Innkeepers   800-231-2639
French, Dutch, and some German spoken   FAX 760-325-8610
WEBSITE www.palmsprings.com/hotels/casacody

LOCATION	From I-5, take the Highway 111 exit, which becomes Palm Canyon Drive. Drive to the center of town and turn right just after the Hyatt Regency onto Tahquitz Canyon. Drive 2 blocks and turn left onto Cahuilla Road.
OPEN	All year
DESCRIPTION	An early California adobe hacienda with southwestern and desert decor, nestled against the San Jacinto Mountains.
NO. OF ROOMS	Twenty-four rooms with private bathrooms.
RATES	Mid-December through April, rates are $79-139 for a single or double. July through September, rates are $49-89 for a single or double. Spring and fall rates are slightly less than high season. There is a two-night minimum stay on weekends, and cancellation requires 72 hours' notice.
CREDIT CARDS	American Express, Diners Club, Discover, MasterCard, Visa
BREAKFAST	Continental plus breakfast is served poolside and includes juice, fruit, hot and cold cereals, English and sweet muffins, and coffee.
AMENITIES	All rooms with air conditioning, private telephone with voice mail, cable TV; all but two rooms have fully equipped kitchens; twelve rooms have private patios and/or fireplaces; two pools; tree-shaded, secluded whirlpool spa.
RESTRICTIONS	Smoking is discouraged in rooms. Cody is the resident Maine coon cat.
MEMBER	California Association of Bed & Breakfast Innkeepers
RATED	AAA 2 Diamonds, Best Places to Kiss 2.5 Lips, Mobil 2 Stars

CASITAS LAQUITA—FOR WOMEN ONLY

450 E Palm Canyon Drive, Palm Springs, CA 92264   760-416-9999
          877-203-3410

COYOTE INN

234 South Patencio Road, Palm Springs, CA 92262   *760-327-0304*
                                                                    888-334-0633

DESERT HILLS HOTEL

601 W Arenas Road, Palm Springs, CA 92262   *760-325-2777*
Joan & Alan Petty, Innkeepers   *800-350-2527*
German spoken   *FAX 760-325-6423*
EMAIL deshils@aol.com   *WEBSITE www.deshills.com*

LOCATION	Take Palm Canyon Road to the center of Palm Springs, turn west (toward the mountain) onto Arenas Road, and drive 5 blocks.
OPEN	All year
DESCRIPTION	A 1960 modern single-story hotel.
NO. OF ROOMS	All rooms with private bathrooms.
RATES	December 15 through May, rates are $75-100 for a single or double and $135-170 for a suite. June to December 14, rates are $65-90 for a single or double and $100-150 for a suite. There is no minimum stay, and cancellation requires notice.
CREDIT CARDS	American Express, Discover, MasterCard, Visa
BREAKFAST	Continental breakfast is served and includes coffee, fresh fruit, sweet rolls, and muffins.
AMENITIES	Bicycles, barbecues, morning newspaper.
RESTRICTIONS	No smoking, no pets, no children.
REVIEWED	*Karen Brown's California: Charming Inns & Itineraries*
RATED	AAA 3 Diamonds

EL MIRASOL VILLAS

525 Warm Sands Drive, Palm Springs, CA 92264   *760-327-5913*
WEBSITE www.elmirasol.com   *800-327-2985*

HACIENDA EN SUENO

586 *Warm Sands Drive, Palm Springs, CA 92264*   760-327-8111
WEBSITE *www.thehacienda.com*   800-359-2007

INGLESIDE INN

200 *West Ramon Road, Palm Springs, CA 92264*   760-325-0046
Melvyn Haber, Innkeeper   800-772-6655
Spanish spoken   FAX 760-325-0710
WEBSITE *www.inglesideinn.com*

LOCATION	At the corner of Ramon Road and Belardo Road, between Palm Canyon Drive and the San Jacinto Mountains, and within walking distance of downtown.
OPEN	All year
DESCRIPTION	A 1925 Spanish hacienda estate with antique furnishings.
NO. OF ROOMS	Thirty rooms with private bathrooms.
RATES	October through June, rates are $95-235 for a single or double and suites are $245-600. July through September, midweek rates are discounted 25 percent. There is a two-night minimum stay on weekends, three nights during holiday weekends. Cancellation requires 48 hours' notice.
CREDIT CARDS	American Express, Diners Club, Discover, MasterCard, Visa
BREAKFAST	Continental breakfast is served in the guestrooms or poolside on the verandah and includes juices, coffee, tea, Danish, muffins, toast, and croissants. Lunch, dinner, and special meals are also available.
AMENITIES	Steam showers, whirlpool tubs in all rooms; 24-hour heated pool and Jacuzzi; robes upon request; room and pool service; piano bar lounge with dancing; coffee-makers in rooms; Melvyn's Restaurant; meeting facilities; mini-refrigerators stocked with complimentary snacks and beverages; fireplaces in most rooms.
RESTRICTIONS	No pets. Children over 12 are welcome.
REVIEWED	*Karen Brown's California: Charming Inns & Itineraries, Fodor's, Frommer's, Dream Resorts, Elegant Small Hotels*
RATED	AAA 3 Diamonds

INN EXILE

960 Camino Parocela, Palm Springs, CA 92262　　760-327-6413
WEBSITE www.innexile.com　　800-962-0186

INNTIMATE

556 Warm Sands Drive, Palm Springs, CA 92264　　760-778-8334
　　800-695-3846

INNTRIGUE

526 Warm Sands Drive, Palm Springs, CA 92264　　760-323-7505
Denny Dewberry & Randy Riggs, Resident Managers　　800-798-8781
EMAIL inntrigue@earthlink.com　　FAX 760-323-1055

LOCATION	In the heart of Palm Springs.
OPEN	All year
DESCRIPTION	A renovated late-1950s clothing-optional resort with spacious rooms and mountain views.
NO. OF ROOMS	Twenty-eight rooms with private bathrooms.
RATES	Year-round rates are $75-175 for a double. There is a three-night minimum stay during holiday weekends. Please ask about a cancellation policy.
CREDIT CARDS	American Express, MasterCard, Visa
BREAKFAST	Continental breakfast is served in the courtyard and includes homemade muffins, fruit, cereals, juices, coffee, and tea.
AMENITIES	Two pools, two Jacuzzis, rooms available with full kitchens, TV/VCRs in all rooms, video library.
RESTRICTIONS	No pets
MEMBER	International Gay Travel Association
AWARDS	1997, Excellence Award, *Out & About*

KORAKIA PENSIONE HISTORIC

257 South Patencio Road, Palm Springs, CA 92262   760-864-6411

L'HORIZON GARDEN HOTEL

1050 East Palm Canyon Drive, Palm Springs, CA 92264   760-323-1858
                                                             800-377-7855

KUDOS/COMMENTS   "A true oasis in the desert. At the foot of spectacular Mount San
                 Jacinto."

ORCHID TREE INN

261 South Belardo Road, Palm Springs, CA 92262   760-325-2791

SAKURA BED & BREAKFAST INN

1677 North Viaduct Miraleste, Palm Springs, CA 92262   760-327-0705
George & Fumiko Cebra, Innkeepers
EMAIL sakura@travelb.com
WEBSITE www.travelbase.com/destinations/palm-springs/sakura

OPEN	All year
DESCRIPTION	A Japanese-style inn decorated with Japanese artwork and antique kimonos.
NO. OF ROOMS	Two rooms with private bathrooms and one room shares a bathroom.
RATES	Year-round rates are $45-75 for a single or double. Cancellation requires seven days' notice.
CREDIT CARDS	No
BREAKFAST	Continental breakfast is served and includes fresh bread or croissants, fresh fruit, and beverages. Japanese and vegetarian meals are available upon request.
AMENITIES	Swimming pool, TV, handmade futons, Japanese kimonos and slippers, shiatsu massage.
RESTRICTIONS	No smoking, no pets. There are two resident cats.

THE TERRA COTTA INN

2388 East Racquet Club Road, Palm Springs, CA 92262   *760-322-6059*
Mary Clare & Tom Mulhall, Innkeepers   *800-786-6938*
French and Spanish spoken   *FAX 760-322-4169*
EMAIL tcotta@earthlink.net   *WEBSITE www.sunnyfun.com*

LOCATION	From I-10 eastbound, exit at Highway 111/Palm Springs. Turn left at the second light in town onto Racquet Club Road. Go east 1.7 miles to the inn.
DESCRIPTION	A 1960 modern inn with tropical decor. A luxurious, clothing-optional inn that is "very private, secure, and relaxing."
NO. OF ROOMS	Seventeen rooms with private bathrooms. Try Room 21, with a private patio and sunken tub.
RATES	Year-round rates are $109-139 for a single or double. There is a two-night minimum stay during weekends and holidays, and cancellation requires one week's notice.
CREDIT CARDS	American Express, MasterCard, Visa
BREAKFAST	Full breakfast is served poolside and includes eight kinds of fresh fruit, English muffins, bagels and cream cheese, croissants, pastries, granola, granola bars, yogurt, eggs, orange juice, coffee, and tea. Lunch is also available.
AMENITIES	Heated pool, Jacuzzi spa with mountain views, afternoon refreshments, mist-cooled patio, up-to-date video library and in-room VCRs; all rooms have refrigerator, microwave, in-room coffee-maker, and TV with remote; guest laundry available; barbecue area.
RESTRICTIONS	No pets, no children. Godiva is the resident pooch. "Godiva is extemely gentle and we provide dog treats so you can have her do tricks and feed her."
REVIEWED	*Los Angeles* magazine

TRAVELLERS REPOSE

66920 1st Street, Desert Hot Springs, CA 92240   *760-329-9584*
Marian Relkoff, Innkeeper

LOCATION	Five miles north of I-10. Take Palm Drive north through town to Pierson Boulevard and turn right. Drive 3 blocks and turn left onto 1st Street.
OPEN	September through June

Trevellers Repose, Desert Hot Springs

DESCRIPTION	A 1985 two-story Victorian home with bay and stained-glass windows, oak floors, lace curtains, homemade crafts, "heart" theme, and some antiques.
NO. OF ROOMS	Three rooms with private bathrooms.
RATES	September through June, rates are $85 for a double. There is no minimum stay, and cancellation requires seven days' notice with a $10 fee.
CREDIT CARDS	No
BREAKFAST	Continental plus is served in the dining room and includes juice, fruit, granola, and homemade muffins, scones, cinnamon rolls, and breads with jams and jellies.
AMENITIES	Afternoon tea, air conditioning, hot tub outside, bedtime surprise.
RESTRICTIONS	No smoking inside, no pets, children over 12 are welcome.
REVIEWED	*The Official Guide to American Historic Inns, America's Wonderful Little Hotels & Inns, Bed & Breakfast USA*
RATED	AAA 2 Diamonds

VILLA ROYALE B&B INN

1620 South Indian Trail, Palm Springs, CA 92264   760-327-2314
Greg Purdy, Innkeeper   800-245-2314
Spanish and French spoken   FAX 760-322-3794
EMAIL info@villaroyale.com   WEBSITE www.villaroyale.com

OPEN	All year
DESCRIPTION	A 1947 Mediterranean inn with European decor, spectacular mountain views, two pools, and fragrant gardens.
NO. OF ROOMS	Thirty-one rooms with private bathrooms.
RATES	October through May, rates are $125-185 for a single or double, $180-275 for a one-bedroom suite, and $275-325 for a two-bedroom suite. June through September, rates are $77-140 for a single or double, $130-175 for a one-bedroom suite, and $175-200 for a two-bedroom suite. There is a two-night minimum stay during weekends and high season, and cancellation requires 48 hours' notice.
CREDIT CARDS	American Express, Carte Blanche, Diners Club, Discover, MasterCard, Visa
BREAKFAST	Continental breakfast is served on the lanai and includes assorted pastries, juice, coffee, tea, and fresh fruit. Dinner is available at the on-site restaurant, Europa.
AMENITIES	Some rooms with private patios and spas; some rooms with fireplaces and kitchenettes; two swimming pools and spa; rose garden; air conditioning; safe deposit boxes; cable TV; on-site, award-winning Europa Restaurant and Bar.
RESTRICTIONS	No smoking inside, no pets
REVIEWED	Karen Brown's California: Charming Inns & Itineraries, Elegant Small Hotels—A Connoisseur's Guide, The Best Places to Kiss in Southern California
RATED	AAA 3 Diamonds

THE WILLOWS HISTORIC PALM SPRINGS INN

412 West Tahquitz Canyon Way, Palm Springs, CA 92262   760-320-0771
Tracy Conrad & Paul Marut, Innkeepers   800-966-9597
Spanish spoken   FAX 760-320-0780
EMAIL innkeeper@thewillowspalmsprings.com
WEBSITE www.thewillowspalmsprings.com

LOCATION	From I-10, follow signs to downtown Palm Springs. At the intersection of Palm Canyon Drive and Tahquitz Canyon Way, go directly west for 3 blocks toward Mount San Jacinto. The inn is on the right side of the street across from Le Valleuris restaurant and next to the Desert Museum.
OPEN	All year
DESCRIPTION	A 1927 two-story Italianate Mediterranean villa with striking architecture, mahogany beams, a veranda with frescoed ceilings, and a 50-foot waterfall that spills into a pool just outside the stone-floored dining room. The inn features 1930s European decor and is decorated with live plants and orchids.
NO. OF ROOMS	Eight rooms with private bathrooms. Try the Marion Davies Room.
RATES	October through May, rates are $250-500 for a single or double. June through September, rates are $175-375 for a single or double. There is a two-night minimum stay during weekends, three nights during holiday weekends; cancellation requires seven days' notice.
CREDIT CARDS	American Express, Carte Blanche, Diners Club, Discover, MasterCard, Visa
BREAKFAST	Full gourmet breakfast varies daily and is served in the dining room. Breakfast may include fresh-baked breads and muffins; gourmet coffee and teas; baked eggs in truffle sauce, frittatas, seasoned scrambled eggs, German puffed pancakes, apricot-stuffed French toast, apple sausage, peppered bacon, plus fresh-squeezed juices. Dinner is also available.
AMENITIES	Fine cotton linens, comfortable upholstered furniture, telephones, cable TV, individual climate control, oversized terry robes, turndown service, spectacular vistas, complimentary refreshments served by the pool, nightly reception with complimentary hors d'oeuvres and wine, limited handicapped accessibility.
RESTRICTIONS	No smoking, no pets, children over 16 are welcome.
REVIEWED	*Fodor's—America's Best Hotels and Restaurants; The National Trust Guide to Historic Bed & Breakfasts, Inns, and Small Hotels; Karen Brown's California: Charming Inns & Itineraries; Bed & Breakfast in California; America's Wonderful Little Hotels and Inns; Recommended Country Inns; The Best Places to Kiss in Southern California; Selected Hotels & Inns North America—The Definitive Guide*
MEMBER	Professional Association of Innkeepers International, California Bed & Breakfast Association
RATED	AAA 4 Diamonds, Mobil 4 Stars
AWARDS	1998, 50 Best Kept Secrets of 1998, *Travel Holiday* magazine; January/February 1999, One of the Top 10 Inns in the Country, *Country Inns* magazine

PASADENA

Everything comes up roses in this town. Pasadena plays host to the Rose Parade and Rose Bowl—the granddaddy of all college football games. It is also the home of the Tournament House, William Wrigley's former mansion and headquarters of the Tournament of Roses Association. The prestigious California Institute of Technology calls Pasadena home, as does the Norton Simon Museum of Art and the Huntington Library. Pasadena is about a dozen miles northeast of downtown Los Angeles in the San Gabriel Valley.

ARTISTS' INN

1038 Magnolia Street, South Pasadena, CA 91030   626-799-5668
Captain Richard & Joey Gurlay, Innkeepers   888-799-5668
French and some German spoken   *FAX 626-799-3678*
EMAIL *artistsinn@artistsinns.com*   WEBSITE *www.artistsinns.com*

LOCATION	Five minutes from old town Pasadena, 10 minutes from downtown LA, 15 minutes from the Burbank Airport, and 20 minutes from Hollywood.
OPEN	All year
DESCRIPTION	A two-story inn surrounded by a white picket fence and decorated with theme rooms.
NO. OF ROOMS	Nine rooms with private bathrooms.
RATES	Year-round rates are $110-205 for a single or double. Cancellation requires seven days' notice.
CREDIT CARDS	American Express, MasterCard, Visa
BREAKFAST	Full gourmet breakfast is served in the dining room or on the porch and features a rotating menu. Special dietary needs can be accommodated.
AMENITIES	Tea and sweets in the afternoon, amenities basket with bottled water, hand-milled soaps, shampoo, hair dryers, European candies, rose garden, canopy beds, Jacuzzi tubs, fireplaces.
RESTRICTIONS	No smoking, no pets, ask about children.
MEMBER	California Hotel & Motel Association, California Association of Bed & Breakfast Inns, Professional Association of Innkeepers International

BISSELL HOUSE BED & BREAKFAST

201 Orange Grove Avenue, South Pasadena, CA 91030   626-441-3535
Russell & Leonore Butcher, Innkeepers   800-441-3530
Spanish spoken   FAX 626-441-3671
WEBSITE *bbchannel.com/bbc/p213422.asp*

LOCATION	Midway between Pasadena and South Pasadena.
OPEN	All year
DESCRIPTION	An expansive Victorian mansion situated at the end of Millionaires Row on a half-acre corner lot enclosed by a 40-foot hedge.
NO. OF ROOMS	Five rooms with private bathrooms.
RATES	Year-round rates are $115-165 for a double. Additional guests are $30 each. There is a two-night minimum stay on weekends, and cancellation requires one week's notice.
CREDIT CARDS	American Express, MasterCard, Visa
BREAKFAST	Full breakfast is served in the dining room and includes fresh-roasted coffee, homemade breads, and a hot entrée that may include the B&B's signature dish, winter French toast. Special meals are available by arrangement.
AMENITIES	Afternoon tea, dessert, non-alcoholic beverage or wine and cheese, handicapped accessible, clawfoot tubs, air conditioning, robes, complimentary beverages.
RESTRICTIONS	No smoking inside, no pets, the B&B is not suitable for children.
MEMBER	California Association of Bed & Breakfast Inns
RATED	AAA 3 Diamonds

PASADENA HOTEL BED & BREAKFAST

76 North Fair Oaks Avenue, Pasadena, CA 91103   626-568-8172

PASO ROBLES

With over 40 wineries in the area, Paso Robles has much to celebrate. The March Zinfandel, Paderewski, May Wine, and October Harvest Festivals all tout the gift of the grape. Other events include the Vine Street Showcase in December, the Kustom Kar Show over Memorial and Labor Day weekends, Concerts in the Park during the summer, and the California Mid-State Fair in August. Paso Robles is about 21 miles north of San Luis Obispo on Highway 101.

ARBOR INN

2130 Arbor Road, Paso Robles, CA 93446   805-227-4673
Denise Mertens, Innkeeper   FAX 805-227-1112
WEBSITE www.bbclub.com/bbc/p500490.asp

OPEN	All year
DESCRIPTION	A two-story English-style home surrounded by an 80-acre vineyard.
NO. OF ROOMS	Nine rooms with private bathrooms.
RATES	Please inquire about current rates and cancellation information.
CREDIT CARDS	MasterCard, Visa
BREAKFAST	Full gourmet breakfast is served.
AMENITIES	Handicapped accessible, fireplaces, balconies, appetizers and wine, evening snacks.
RESTRICTIONS	No smoking, no pets, children over 11 are welcome.
MEMBER	Professional Association of Innkeepers International, California Association of Bed & Breakfast Inns

GILLIE ARCHER INN

1433 Oak Street, Paso Robles, CA 93446   805-238-0879
EMAIL gillie@tcsn.net   FAX 805-238-2516
WEBSITE www.virtualcities.com

LOCATION	Traveling north on Highway 101, take the first off ramp, Spring Street, and continue north on Spring to 14th Street. Make a left on 14th, go 1 block to Oak Street, and make a right. Travelling south on 101, take the first off ramp, Spring Street, and continue on Spring to 15th. Make a right, go 1 block to Oak Street, and make a left.
OPEN	All year

DESCRIPTION	A 1917 two-story transitional Craftsman with maple floors, clear cedar built-ins throughout, and a flowing floorplan, decorated with comfortable elegance, with some antiques and Persian carpets.
NO. OF ROOMS	Two rooms with private bathrooms and three rooms share one bathroom. Try the Fireplace Room in the winter and the Children's Room in the summer.
RATES	May through January 1, rates are $150-165 for a single or double with a private bathroom and $95-105 for a single or double with a shared bathroom. January 2 through April, rates are $135-150 for a single or double with a private bathroom and $90-95 for a single or double with a shared bathroom. There is a minimum stay during festivals and extended holiday weekends. Cancellation requires eight days' notice.
CREDIT CARDS	American Express, Discover, MasterCard, Visa
BREAKFAST	Continental breakfast is served in the dining room and includes fresh-squeezed juice, fresh fruit, and homemade pastries.
AMENITIES	Afternoon tea, fresh flowers in all the rooms and throughout the house, robes, air conditioning, wood-burning fireplaces in the living room and one bedroom, gazebo with stained glass in the yard, beautiful garden with fountain, all rooms with TV/VCRs, video library, within walking distance of restaurants and antique stores and centrally located to many fine wineries.
RESTRICTIONS	No smoking, no pets, children over 11 are welcome.
REVIEWED	*Fodor's*

JUST INN

11680 Chimney Rock Road, Paso Robles, CA 93446   805-238-6932

SUMMIT CREEK RANCH

6350 Peachy Canyon Road, Paso Robles, CA 93446   805-237-1870
EMAIL *info@summitcreekranch.com*
WEBSITE *www.summitcreekranch.com*

LOCATION	In the Paso Robles wine district.
OPEN	All year
DESCRIPTION	An early California adobe-style ranch house decorated with a traditional Mexican theme and contemporary luxury.

RATES	Please inquire about current rates and cancellation information.
BREAKFAST	Continental breakfast is served in the dining room.
AMENITIES	Afternoon wine and cheese.

POSEY

Outdoor enthusiasts will find plenty to do around Posey. Fish Poso Creek, or hike and hunt in the Sequoia National Forest. Nearby Glennville hosts the annual rodeo during the first weekend in June.

PANORAMA HEIGHTS BED & BREAKFAST

45758 Guhl Avenue, Posey, CA 93260   661-536-8971
Greg & Debbie Boshears, Innkeepers   FAX 661-536-8738
EMAIL *panoramaheights@mail-me.com*

LOCATION	Take Highway 99 to Highway 155 and travel east 35.1 miles. Turn left onto Jack Ranch Road, drive 5.5 miles, and turn right onto Old Stage Drive. Go 5.9 miles to Guhl Avenue and Booth Street.
OPEN	All year
DESCRIPTION	A 1948 two-story traditional country host home with country decor. An old, spacious mountain lodge, transformed to reflect a relaxed, cozy atmosphere. Maple trees and aged redwoods, flower and vegetable gardens accent the manicured grounds.
NO. OF ROOMS	Four rooms with private bathrooms.
RATES	May through September, rates are $75 for a single or double during midweek and $85 on weekends and holidays. October through April, rates are $65 for a single or double during midweek and $85 on weekends and holidays. There is no minimum stay, and cancellation requires 48 hours' notice.
CREDIT CARDS	No
BREAKFAST	Full breakfast is served in the dining room and includes eggs, potatoes, bacon or sausage, fruit, bread, coffee, tea, juice, and milk. Cereal is served upon request. Lunch and dinner are also available.
AMENITIES	Refrigerator, microwave in library, flowers in bedrooms, satellite TV/VCR, stereo system, large rock fireplace in living room, evening snack, large decks in front and back, barbecue, horseshoe pit.
RESTRICTIONS	No smoking. Charlie Brown and Lucy are the resident pooches; Zee is the calico. "The African Grey parrot welcomes visitors."
REVIEWED	*Bed & Breakfast Southern California*

Panorama Heights Bed & Breakfast, Posey

RAMONA

This small town lies between Escondido and Julian, on the high road to Anza-Borrego Desert State Park, on the outskirts of Cleveland National Forest. San Diego is a scant 30 miles south.

LAKE SUTHERLAND LODGE BED & BREAKFAST

24901 Dam Oaks Drive, Ramona, CA 92065
Jon & Diana Rogers, Innkeepers
EMAIL *diana@loglodge.com*
WEBSITE *www.loglodge.com*

760-789-6483
800-789-6483
FAX 760-788-9832

LOCATION	From Ramona, take Highway 78 east 6 miles, turn north on Sutherland Dam Road, and go 1.3 miles to Dam Oaks Drive.
OPEN	All year
DESCRIPTION	A 1994 two-story lodge of lodgepole pine construction with river stone fireplaces in the Great Room.
NO. OF ROOMS	Four rooms with private bathrooms.
RATES	Year-round rates are $110-205 for a single or double. There is a minimum stay during weekends and holidays. Cancellation requires 14 days' notice.
CREDIT CARDS	American Express, Discover, MasterCard, Visa

BREAKFAST	Full gourmet breakfast is served in the dining room.
AMENITIES	Feather beds, private bathrooms, in-room coffee and tea, robes, hot tubs, air conditioning, fishing, horseback riding (extra fee), fireplaces in Great Room and Honeymoon Suite.
RESTRICTIONS	No smoking, no pets, no children. There are dogs, cats, and horses on the property.
REVIEWED	*Romantic Julian, Romantic San Diego, Sunset* magazine
MEMBER	California Lodging Industry Association, California Association of Bed & Breakfast Inns
RATED	AAA 3 Diamonds

RANCHO CUCAMONGA

CHRISTMAS HOUSE BED & INN

9240 Archibald Avenue, Rancho Cucamonga, CA 91730   *909-980-6450*

RANDSBURG

Just east of the El Paso Mountains, Randsburg is surrounded by bone-dry lakes. Bring your moisturizer to this desert town. From here, you are moments from Red Rock Canyon Park and a short drive from Death Valley. The Balloon Festival, just north in Ridgecrest, gets under way in November.

COTTAGE HOTEL BED & BREAKFAST

130 Butte Avenue, Randsburg, CA 93554   *760-374-2285*
Bill & Brenda Ingram, Innkeepers   *888-268-4622*
WEBSITE www.randsburg.com   *FAX 760-374-2132*

LOCATION	Twenty-two miles from Ridgecrest, between Highways 395 and 14, 1 mile off Highway 395 at the top of Butte Avenue.
OPEN	All year
DESCRIPTION	A restored 1900 western hotel constructed of wood and stucco with Victorian decor. Listed on the California Historic Register.

NO. OF ROOMS	Four rooms and a guesthouse with private bathrooms. Try the Lace Room.
RATES	Year-round rates are $75-95 for a single or double and $85-125 for the guesthouse. There is no minimum stay, and cancellation requires 48 hours' notice for a full refund.
CREDIT CARDS	American Express, Discover, MasterCard, Visa
BREAKFAST	Full breakfast is served in the dining room and includes a hot dish such as waffles, pancakes, or biscuits and gravy; cereals; pastries; fruits; juice, milk, Starbuck's coffee, teas, cider, and cocoa.
AMENITIES	Light evening refreshments in the tea room; oversize, enclosed Jacuzzi; private gardens with fountains and benches; ceiling fans; two rooms with balconies; sun room with library and writing desk; cottage with handicapped access.
RESTRICTIONS	No smoking, no pets, children of any age are welcome in the guest cottage. Hillery and Midnight are the resident outdoors cats.
REVIEWED	*The Antique Atlas*
MEMBER	Automobile Bed & Breakfast Association, California Lodging Industry Association
RATED	AAA 2 Diamonds

RED MOUNTAIN

Welcome to true desert country. Dry lakes dot the countryside around Red Mountain, and the sun shines relentlessly. Explore the historical buildings in the Rand Gold Mining District. Check out the annual Fourth of July Old West Festival. Red Mountain is about 20 miles south of Ridgecrest on Highway 395.

OLD OWL INN COTTAGES

701 Highway 395, Red Mountain, CA 93558   760-374-2235
Lynn & Jeanie Walker, Innkeepers   888-653-6954
FAX 760-374-2354

LOCATION	Twenty-five miles north of the junction of Highways 395 and 58.
OPEN	All year
DESCRIPTION	Two cottages built in the 1880s.
NO. OF ROOMS	Three rooms with private bathrooms.
RATES	Year-round rates are $45-55 for a single or double. Additional guests are $10 each. There is no minimum stay, and cancellation requires 48 hours' notice.

CREDIT CARDS	Discover, MasterCard, Visa
BREAKFAST	Breakfast baskets are delivered to the guestrooms and include juice, fruit, baked goods, and hot drinks.
AMENITIES	Snack basket with sparkling cider served upon arrival, fenced-in yards, barbecues, picnic area. Slim's Cottage includes a full kitchen, living room, and old-fashioned bath. Bessie's Honeymoon Cottage includes a kitchenette.
RESTRICTIONS	No smoking. Misty is the resident pooch.
REVIEWED	*The Antique Atlas*
MEMBER	California Lodging Industry Association, Professional Association of Innkeepers International

REEDLEY

FAIRWEATHER INN

259 South Reed Avenue, Reedley, CA 93654   559-638-1918

REEDLEY COUNTRY BED & BREAKFAST

43137 Road 52, Reedley, CA 93654   559-638-2585

RIDGECREST

The southern gateway to Death Valley, Ridgecrest features the Balloon Festival in November, tours of ancient petroglyphs, the Desert Empire Fair, the Spring Festival, and gem and mineral shows. Ridgecrest is on Highway 395 (business route) at the junction with Highway 178.

BEVLEN HAUS BED & BREAKFAST

809 N Sanders Street, Ridgecrest, CA 93555   760-375-1988
Bev & Len de Geus, Innkeepers   800-375-1989
EMAIL *blh_b&b@iwvisp.com*   FAX 760-375-6871

LOCATION	From Highway 14, exit east onto Highway 178 and drive 14 miles to China Lake Boulevard, and at the first stoplight go south 1 mile to Drummond. Take a right, drive 1 block, turn left on North Sanders, and drive 1 block.
OPEN	All year
DESCRIPTION	A ranch-style host home with comfortable traditional furniture and eclectic decor including lots of wood and antiques, situated in California's high desert country.
NO. OF ROOMS	Three rooms with private bathrooms.
RATES	Year-round rates are $45-65 for a single or double. There is no minimum stay. Ask about a cancellation policy.
CREDIT CARDS	American Express, Discover, MasterCard, Visa
BREAKFAST	Full breakfast is served in the dining room and includes fruit, juice, coffee, tea, a hot main dish, assorted homemade breads, rolls, biscuits, muffins, jams, and jellies.
AMENITIES	Air conditioning, ceiling fans in all rooms, hot tub spa, off-street parking, handmade soaps, evening refreshments, champagne for special occasions, old-fashioned kitchen with antique cast-iron wood-burning stove and hand-hammered copper sink; sitting room with another antique wood-burning cookstove.
RESTRICTIONS	No smoking, no pets. Molly is the resident Yorkshire terrier.
REVIEWED	*The Official Guide to American Historic Inns*

RUNNING SPRINGS

In the San Bernardino Mountains, at the junction of Highway 330 and the Rim of the World Drive, Running Springs is perfectly positioned for excursions to Lake Arrowhead, Big Bear Lake, and all points in between.

SPRING OAKS BED & BREAKFAST INN AND MOUNTAIN RETREAT CENTER

2465 Spring Oaks Drive, Running Springs, CA 92382   *909-867-7797*
William Florian, Innkeeper   *800-867-9636*
EMAIL *springoaks@webtv.net*   WEBSITE *springoaks.com*

LOCATION	Near Lake Arrowhead, 1 mile west of the center of Running Springs just off Highway 18. Turn south on Glen View, then left on Spring Oak. Ninety miles east of Los Angeles.
OPEN	All year
DESCRIPTION	A 1955 two-story mountain lodge with rustic, knotty pine interior and exposed beams, surrounded by forest on a ridge with 100-mile views.
NO. OF ROOMS	One room with a private bathroom and two rooms share one bathroom.
RATES	Year-round rates are $120-130 for a single or double with a private bathroom and $85-95 for a single or double with a shared bathroom. There are discounts for multinight stays. There is no minimum stay, and cancellation requires 72 hours' notice.
CREDIT CARDS	MasterCard, Visa
BREAKFAST	Full healthy, natural breakfast is served.
AMENITIES	Hiking, remote wilderness hot springs, clothing-optional hot tub.
RESTRICTIONS	No smoking, no pets, children over seven are welcome. Sassie is the resident cat; Sammie is the dog.

SAN CLEMENTE

About 20 miles south of Newport Beach on Highway 101, San Clemente is among Southern California's best seaside playgrounds. Its State Beach is one of the least crowded and most beautiful around, and Richard Nixon's grand estate can still be seen perched atop a cliff. Cyclists will enjoy the 20-mile stretch from here to Camp Pendleton.

CASA TROPICANA BED & BREAKFAST

610 Avenida Victoria, San Clemente, CA 92672   714-492-1234
Rick & Christy Anderson, Innkeepers   800-492-1245
WEBSITE www.casatropicana.com   FAX 714-492-2423

OPEN	All year
DESCRIPTION	A three-story Southwest-style host home decorated with a tropical theme.
NO. OF ROOMS	Nine rooms with private bathrooms.
RATES	Year-round rates are $95-350 for double. Ask about a cancellation policy.
CREDIT CARDS	American Express, MasterCard, Visa
BREAKFAST	Full breakfast is served.
AMENITIES	Ocean views, fireplaces, Jacuzzi tubs, queen- and king-size beds, refrigerator.
RESTRICTIONS	Smoking outside only, no pets, accommodations are not suitable for children.
MEMBER	California Association of Bed & Breakfast Inns

SAN DIEGO

California's second-largest city boasts beautiful beaches, with some 70 miles of coastline stretching from the north of town down to the Mexican border. Beyond sun and sand, other major draws to the area include Sea World, Old Town San Diego, the Gaslamp Quarter, the San Diego Zoo and Balboa Park, LegoLand, San Diego Wild Animal Park, the Maritime Museum, and Seaport Village. Outdoor concerts abound in summer and theater entertains during the balmy winter. Tijuana, Mexico, is about 20 miles to the south.

BALBOA PARK INN

3402 Park Boulevard, San Diego, CA 92103   619-298-0823
Edward Wilcox, Innkeeper   800-938-8181
Spanish spoken   FAX 619-294-8070
EMAIL *info@BalboaParkInn.com*   WEBSITE *www.balboaparkinn.com*

OPEN	All year
DESCRIPTION	Four two-story Spanish colonial buildings in a quiet neighborhood in central San Diego.
NO. OF ROOMS	Twenty-six suites with private bathrooms.
RATES	Please inquire about current rates and cancellation information.
CREDIT CARDS	American Express, Diners Club, Discover, MasterCard, Visa
BREAKFAST	Continental plus breakfast is delivered to the guestrooms.
AMENITIES	Queen-size beds, refrigerators, coffee-makers, daily newspaper, cable TV with HBO.
RESTRICTIONS	No pets, children are welcome.
MEMBER	California Association of Bed & Breakfast Inns

BAY BREEZE BED & BREAKFAST

3032 Serbian Place, San Diego, CA 92117   619-275-3995
Joe & Gwen Schobert, Innkeepers
German spoken
WEBSITE *www.bbchannel.com/bbc/p150293.asp*

OPEN	All year
DESCRIPTION	A three-story contemporary host home, overlooking Mission Bay Park and the night lights of the city, decorated with collectibles culled from the innkeepers' world travels.

NO. OF ROOMS	One room with a private bathroom.
RATES	Year-round rates are $85-125 for a single or double. A minimum stay is required, and cancellation requires five days' notice.
CREDIT CARDS	Discover, MasterCard, Visa
BREAKFAST	Full healthy breakfast is served in the dining room. Special meals are available with prior arrangement.
AMENITIES	Orchid garden gazebo, afternoon tea.
RESTRICTIONS	No smoking, no pets, the accommodations are not suitable for children.

BEACH HUT

PO Box 90334, San Diego, CA 92169   619-272-6131
Billee J. York, Innkeeper   FAX 619-483-3671
EMAIL Billee@aol.com
WEBSITE www.ncbbi.org/inns/A003986.html or
www.virtualcities.com/vacation/ca/x/cax47v3.htm

OPEN	All year
DESCRIPTION	A cozy beach cottage with a lovely garden, located in a pleasant residential neighborhood in the Pacific Beach area of San Diego. The cottage looks out on Mission Bay.
NO. OF ROOMS	One room with a private bathroom.
RATES	Year-round rates are $95 per night and $575 per week. There is a two-night minimum stay, and cancellation requires two weeks' notice.
CREDIT CARDS	No
BREAKFAST	The kitchen is fully stocked with breakfast items.
AMENITIES	Four-poster bed, fully equipped kitchen, cable TV, air conditioning, radio, telephone, down comforters, patio, swimming pool, coffee and tea service.
RESTRICTIONS	No smoking, no pets. The cottage accommodates a maximum of two guests.
MEMBER	Bed & Breakfast Guild of San Diego

BLOM HOUSE BED & BREAKFAST

4600 Kensington Drive, San Diego, CA 92116   619-282-2262
Bette Blom, Innkeeper   800-797-2566
EMAIL BlomHouse@aol.com   FAX 619-467-0890
WEBSITE www.virtualcities.com/ons/ca/x/cax1901.htm

OPEN	All year
DESCRIPTION	A 1927 two-story Spanish-style host home with hardwood floors and beamed ceilings, located in a historic neighborhood.
NO. OF ROOMS	Four rooms with private bathrooms.
RATES	Please inquire about current rates and cancellation information.
CREDIT CARDS	MasterCard, Visa
BREAKFAST	Full breakfast is served and includes homemade granola, fresh fruit, a hot entrée, and beverages.
AMENITIES	Air conditioning; TV/VCR; refrigerators; wine, cheese, and crackers; close to shopping, a park, and a vintage movie theater.
RESTRICTIONS	Smoking outside only, pets welcome by prior arrangement .

THE BLUE DOOR BED & BREAKFAST

13707 Durango Drive, Del Mar, CA 92014   858-755-3819
Robert & Anna Belle Schock, Innkeepers

LOCATION	Twenty miles north of San Diego, overlooking Torrey Pines State Reserve.
OPEN	All year
DESCRIPTION	A 1971 host home, uniquely designed specifically for its owners; remodeled and refurbished in 1993.
NO. OF ROOMS	A two-room suite with a private bathroom.
RATES	Year-round rates are $70-80 for a double. There is no minimum stay required. Ask about a cancellation policy.
CREDIT CARDS	No
BREAKFAST	Full breakfast is served in the country kitchen or dining room and includes home-baked goods and an entrée such as orange French toast.
AMENITIES	Fresh flowers, TV/VCR, sitting room, refrigerator, patio with great views.

RESTRICTIONS   No smoking, no pets, ask about children.
REVIEWED   *Bed & Breakfast USA*

BUENA VISTA BED & BREAKFAST

5446 Candlelight Drive, La Jolla, CA 92037   *619-454-9646*
Niels & Renate Stoermer, Innkeepers   *FAX 619-454-5360*
Spanish, French, and German spoken
EMAIL *rstoermer@compuserve.com*
WEBSITE *www.bbonline.com/ca/buenavista/*

OPEN	All year
DESCRIPTION	A Mediterranean-style host home decorated with unique furnishings and artwork, located in an exclusive neighborhood in La Jolla.
NO. OF ROOMS	Two rooms with private bathrooms.
RATES	Year-round rates are $95-105 for a single or double. There is a two-night minimum stay. Ask about a cancellation policy.
BREAKFAST	Full breakfast is served in the breakfast room or on the terrace and includes a hot entrée, tea, coffee, and hot chocolate.
AMENITIES	Afternoon tea, pool, spa, city and ocean views, king-size beds, private entrances.
RESTRICTIONS	Smoking outside only, no pets, children over 12 are welcome.

CAPTAIN MIKE'S BED BRUNCH & SAILING

2040 Harbor Island Drive, San Diego, CA 92101   *619-297-9692*
Mike Griffin, Innkeeper
Some French and Spanish spoken
EMAIL *capnmike66@netscape.net*

LOCATION	Just south of the San Diego airport at Harbor Island West Marina, on the west end of Harbor Island. The entrance to the island is right in front of the airport entrance. There is plenty of free parking at the marina.
OPEN	All year
DESCRIPTION	Yachts ranging in size from 35 to 46 feet long, both power and sail boats, most accommodating up to seven people.
NO. OF ROOMS	Yachts with private bathrooms.

RATES	May through September, rates are $70 for a double plus $15 per additional person. October through April, rates are $60 for a single or double plus $15 per additional person. There is no minimum stay but multinight stays are discounted $10 for each night after the first. Cancellation requires seven days' notice for a full refund.
CREDIT CARDS	No
BREAKFAST	Guests are given coupons worth $5 to be used toward brunch at either the marina Deli or the Waterfront Cafe at the Travelodge located next to the marina. The deli has a varied, hearty, simple breakfast menu that can usually be purchased in full with the coupon provided. The Waterfront Cafe has a full breakfast menu and a full buffet. Guests are responsible for all charges over the amount of the $5 coupon.
AMENITIES	All yachts are equipped with refrigeration, toilets, heaters, and stereos; some have showers, and TV/VCRs ($5 extra charge for these yachts); some yachts have microwave ovens. No other cooking is permitted. The marina has shower and sauna facilities, and an unheated swimming pool; guests may also use the heated swimming pool and Jacuzzi at the Travelodge. Discounts on sailing trips; possible scheduled and private-charter sunset sailing tours of San Diego Harbor (June thru August only). "I will also pick up guests at the airport if arrival is after 4 p.m. on weekdays, or before 11 a.m. on weekends." The marina is centrally located to all of San Diego's tourist attractions.
RESTRICTIONS	No smoking, no pets. No loud noise in the marina after 10 p.m.; no cooking (except microwave) on any yacht; no extra overnight guests.

CAROLE'S BED & BREAKFAST INN

3227 Grim Avenue, San Diego, CA 92104   619-280-5258
Carole Dugdale, Innkeeper   800-975-5521
Spanish spoken
EMAIL *carolesbnb@hotmail.com*
WEBSITE *www.virtualcities.com/%7Evirtual/ons/ca/x/cax35040.htm*

LOCATION	Take I-5 south to the Pershing exit. Follow Pershing around the golf course. At the top of the hill, turn right onto Redwood. Stay on Redwood until 1 block past the light. Turn left onto Grim Avenue. Look for the picket fence and large American flag.
OPEN	All year
DESCRIPTION	A 1904 two-story early California Craftsman-style bungalow with hardwood floors and lots of antiques, located in the historic district near Balboa Park.

Carole's Bed & Breakfast Inn, San Diego

NO. OF ROOMS	Four rooms with private bathrooms and six rooms share bathrooms. Carole recommends the Mayor's Room.
RATES	Year-round rates are $89-99 for a single or double with a private bathroom, $69 for a single or double with a shared bathroom, $159 for a two-bedroom suite, and $109 for the guesthouse. There is no minimum stay, and cancellation requires seven days' notice.
CREDIT CARDS	American Express, Discover, MasterCard, Visa
BREAKFAST	Continental plus is served in the dining room and includes fresh tropical fruit, fresh-squeezed juice, homemade breads and muffins, a baked egg dish or hot cereal, fresh-ground coffee, and herbal tea.
AMENITIES	Swimming pool, hot tub, coffee and tea available at all times, garden, decks.
RESTRICTIONS	No smoking inside, no pets
REVIEWED	*Inn & Travel*
MEMBER	San Diego Bed & Breakfast Guild

THE COTTAGE

3829 Albatross Street, San Diego, CA 92103   *619-299-1564*
Robert & Carol Emerick, Innkeepers   *FAX 619-299-6213*
EMAIL cemerick@adnc.com   *WEBSITE www.sandiegobandb.com*

LOCATION	From I-5, take the Washington Street exit. Follow Washington Street to 1st Avenue, turn right, and drive 2 blocks to Robinson. Turn right, go 2 blocks, and turn onto Albatross.
OPEN	All year
DESCRIPTION	A 1913 two-story homestead-style main house and a 1942 cottage decorated with period and contemporary furnishings. The cottage is furnished with walnut and oak period pieces.
NO. OF ROOMS	Two rooms with private bathrooms.
RATES	Year-round rates are $65-105 for a single or double. There is a minimum stay, and cancellation requires seven days' notice for a refund less a $10 fee.
CREDIT CARDS	American Express, Discover, MasterCard, Visa
BREAKFAST	Continental breakfast is served in the dining room or guestrooms and includes fresh-baked breads, fresh fruit, and a beverage from the local roaster.
AMENITIES	Each room shares a garden and has a telephone, TV, and refrigerator.
RESTRICTIONS	No smoking inside, no pets
REVIEWED	*Frommer's, Fodor's, Best Places to Stay in California, The Best Places to Kiss in Southern California, Bed & Breakfast USA*
MEMBER	San Diego Bed & Breakfast Guild

CRONE'S COBBLESTONE COTTAGE

1302 Washington Place, San Diego, CA 92103   *619-295-4765*

DMITRI'S

931 21st Street, San Diego, CA 92102   *619-238-5547*
Elayna Mootry, Innkeeper

LOCATION	Take I-5 south to Highway 94 east, exit onto G Street, turn left onto 22nd, turn left on Broadway, and left again onto 21st Street.

OPEN	All year
DESCRIPTION	A two-story guesthouse.
NO. OF ROOMS	Three rooms with private bathrooms and two rooms share one bathroom.
RATES	Year-round rates are $75 for a single or double with a private bathroom and $65 for a single or double with a shared bathroom. There is a minimum stay, and cancellation requires 14 days' notice.
CREDIT CARDS	MasterCard, Visa
BREAKFAST	Continental breakfast includes fruit, pastry, tea, coffee, milk, cereal, and orange juice.
AMENITIES	Bikes, pool, spa, surfing equipment, wet suits.
RESTRICTIONS	No smoking, no pets, no children. Alex is the resident cat.

ELSBREE HOUSE BED & BREAKFAST

5054 Narragansett Avenue, San Diego, CA 92107   619-226-4133
800-510-6975 *(message service)*
FAX 619-223-4133

LOCATION	Half a block from the beach in the Ocean Beach community.
DESCRIPTION	A 1991 two-story New England–style host home.
NO. OF ROOMS	All rooms with private bathrooms.
RATES	Please inquire about current rates and cancellation information.
CREDIT CARDS	MasterCard, Visa
BREAKFAST	Continental breakfast is served.
AMENITIES	Flowers, fireplaces, TV, hair dryers, iron and ironing board, patio, balconies.
RESTRICTIONS	No smoking, no pets, children are welcome.
REVIEWED	*The Best Places to Kiss in Southern California*

ERENE'S BED & BREAKFAST

3776 Hawk Street, San Diego, CA 92103   619-295-5622

Harbor Hill Guest House

2330 Albatross Street, San Diego, CA 92101   619-233-0638

Heritage Park Bed & Breakfast

2470 Heritage Park Row, San Diego, CA 92110   619-299-6832
EMAIL innkeeper@heritageparkinn.com   800-995-2470
WEBSITE www.heritageparkinn.com   FAX 619-299-9465

LOCATION	In San Diego's historic Old Town district.
OPEN	All year
DESCRIPTION	A restored 1889 two-story Victorian inn with large porch; listed on the National Historic Register.
NO. OF ROOMS	Twelve rooms with private bathrooms.
RATES	Please inquire about current rates. There is a two-night minimum stay during weekends, three nights during holiday weekends; cancellation requires seven days' notice.
CREDIT CARDS	American Express, Discover, MasterCard, Visa
BREAKFAST	Full gourmet breakfast is served in the dining room or on the veranda. Dinner and special meals are available on request.
AMENITIES	Afternoon tea and fruit, feather beds, robes, clawfoot tubs, turndown service, homemade cookies, fax and copier, Jacuzzi, library, tea and coffee available all day, handicapped accessible.
RESTRICTIONS	No smoking inside, no pets
MEMBER	Professional Association of Innkeepers International, California Association of Bed & Breakfast Inns
KUDOS/COMMENTS	"Lovely historic buildings in city-operated park, known for breakfast setting and late afternoon tea." "A gem in the historic part of town."

Keating House

2331 2nd Avenue, San Diego, CA 92101   619-239-8585

PLUM TREE COTTAGE

4220 St. James Place, San Diego, CA 92103   *619-291-2930*

RIVIERA BED & BREAKFAST

3835 Riviera Drive, San Diego, CA 92109   *619-483-4878*
Trisha Landoni, Innkeeper
Spanish, Italian, and German spoken
EMAIL Riviera@beachpad.net
WEBSITE www.beachpad.net

LOCATION	Approximately 7 miles north of downtown San Diego on Mission Bay, 1 mile north of Sea World. Take the Mission Bay Drive exit off I-8 and drive north for 2 miles, turning left onto Riviera Drive. The B&B is 0.3 mile on the right side.
DESCRIPTION	A 1948 two-story Southern California–style beach house with hardwood floors throughout and traditional decor. The building is surrounded by tropical gardens. A two-story vacation rental with separate entrance is in the back.
NO. OF ROOMS	Two rooms with private bathrooms. Try the Garden Room.
RATES	June through September, rates are $130 for a single or double. October through May, rates are $110 for a single or double. There is a two-night minimum stay, and cancellation requires seven days' notice.
CREDIT CARDS	American Express, MasterCard, Visa
BREAKFAST	Full gourmet breakfast is served on the weekends and continental the rest of the week. Breakfast is served in the dining room or on the tropical patio. Picnic-basket lunches are also available.
AMENITIES	Fresh flowers and robes in each room; across the street from Mission Bay; picnic baskets, beach towels, chairs, and beach umbrellas; telephone; 1 mile from Sea World.
RESTRICTIONS	No smoking, no pets, no children. Avi is the resident calico.

San Diego Yacht & Breakfast

1880 Harbor Island Drive #G dock, San Diego, CA 92101   619-297-9484
Tony Ward & Jack Caple, Innkeepers   800-922-4836
Spanish, Japanese, and Filipino spoken   619-295-9182
EMAIL yachtdo@yachtdo.com   *WEBSITE www.yachtdo.com*

LOCATION	Take I-5 south to Rosecrans. Go 3 miles on Rosecrans to Nimitz, turn left and go 2 miles to Harbor Island. Turn right onto the island and drive 1 mile to Marina Cortez.
OPEN	All year
DESCRIPTION	Various boats, 35 to 68 feet in length, surrounded by 600 other yachts.
NO. OF ROOMS	Yachts with private bathrooms. Try the Chinese Junk.
RATES	May 15 through October 15, rates are $195-350. The remainder of the year, rates are 10 percent less. There is no minimum stay. Rain checks are issued for cancellations.
CREDIT CARDS	American Express, Diners Club, MasterCard, Visa
BREAKFAST	Full breakfast is chosen from the menu at the deli on shore.
AMENITIES	Daily newspaper, fresh flowers.
RESTRICTIONS	No smoking, no pets, children over five are welcome.
REVIEWED	*Country Inns, Frommer's, Mature Traveler*
MEMBER	California Association of Bed & Breakfast Inns, Professional Association of Innkeepers International

Sandcastle Bed & Breakfast

3880 Bayside Walk, San Diego, CA 92109   619-488-3880
Bart & Judy Sayer, Innkeepers   FAX 619-488-7845
WEBSITE www. beachandbay.com

LOCATION	From I-5, take the Garnet exit and head west 2 miles to Mission Boulevard. Turn left (south) and drive about 0.7 mile to San Jose Place. Turn left and drive 1 block to Bayside Lane. Turn left and go about 0.2 mile to Vanitie Court and Bayside Walk.
OPEN	All year
DESCRIPTION	A 1979 three-story post-modern host home situated on Mission Bay.
NO. OF ROOMS	Two rooms with private bathrooms.

RATES	June through September, rates are $125-135 for a single or double. The remainder of the year, rates are $105-115 for a single or double. There is a two-night minimum stay.
CREDIT CARDS	American Express, MasterCard, Visa
BREAKFAST	Continental plus is served in the guestrooms and includes juice, fresh fruit, bread or pastry, and beverages.
AMENITIES	Breathtaking views of Mission Bay, the San Diego skyline, the La Jolla hills, and the Pacific Ocean.
RESTRICTIONS	No smoking, no pets, children over 12 are welcome.
REVIEWED	*Sunset* magazine, *Progressive Architecture*

SAN LUIS OBISPO

Twelve miles inland from the coast via Highway 101, San Luis Obispo is situated in the heart of central California's wine country and is backdropped by the Santa Lucia Mountains. Major events include the acclaimed Mozart Festival in late July and early August, the Wine Festival in September, the Film Festival in November, and the Farmers' Market Street Fair every Thursday.

ADOBE INN

1473 Monterey Street, San Luis Obispo, CA 93401   *805-549-0321*
Jim & Shari Towles, Innkeepers   *800-676-1588*
Spanish spoken   FAX *805-549-0383*
EMAIL *jtowles@aol.com*   WEBSITE *www.abobeinns.com*

LOCATION	Take the California Boulevard exit from Highway 101, take a left on California, and go to the second stoplight. Go right on Monterey and then take an immediate left into the parking lot.
OPEN	All year
DESCRIPTION	A 1950 two-story stucco inn with frame construction and Southwest decor.
NO. OF ROOMS	Fifteen rooms with private bathrooms. Try the Barbadous Room.
RATES	June through August, rates are $65-110 for a single or double. December through February, rates are $55-75 for a single or double. There is no minimum stay, and cancellation requires 48 hours' notice.
CREDIT CARDS	American Express, Discover, MasterCard, Visa

BREAKFAST	Full breakfast is served buffet style in the dining room and includes homemade granola, muesli, and cornflakes with fresh fruit, homemade breads and muffins, English muffins, jam and applebutter, and a different hot item served from the kitchen such as waffles, quiche, or pancakes.
AMENITIES	Air conditioning; free local calls; meeting facilities; rooms individually decorated, many with kitchenettes; lovely cactus patio.
RESTRICTIONS	No smoking, no pets
REVIEWED	*Fodor's*
MEMBER	California Lodging Industry Association

GARDEN STREET INN

1212 Garden Street, San Luis Obispo, CA 93401   *805-545-9802*
EMAIL *InnKeeper@GardenStreetInn.com*   *800-488-2045*
WEBSITE *www.gardenstreetinn.com*   *FAX 805-545-9403*

LOCATION	Two hundred miles north of Los Angeles off Highway 101.
DESCRIPTION	A restored 1887 Italianate–Queen Anne inn decorated with antiques and period decor.
NO. OF ROOMS	Nine rooms with private bathrooms.
RATES	Please inquire about current rates and cancellation information. A two-night minimum stay is required during holidays and special events; cancellation requires seven days' notice.
CREDIT CARDS	American Express, Discover, MasterCard, Visa
BREAKFAST	Full breakfast is served in the breakfast room.
AMENITIES	Evening wine and cheese; all rooms have fireplaces, armoires, queen- or king-size beds; hot tubs; library.
RESTRICTIONS	No smoking inside, no pets, children over 15 are welcome.
KUDOS/COMMENTS	"Great place. In the center of town."

HERITAGE INN

978 Olive Street, San Luis Obispo, CA 93405   *805-544-7440*

SAN SIMEON

A beautiful 9 miles north of Cambria on Highway 1, San Simeon sits on the lovely bay of the same name, just a short distance from the famous Hearst Castle and Historic Monument. Tour the local wineries, fish from the pier, stroll along the beach, or just watch the elephant seals lounge about.

SEBASTIAN'S BED & BREAKFAST

442 SLO San Simeon Road, San Simeon, CA 93452   805-927-4217
EMAIL sebastians@thegrid.net   FAX 805-927-1660
WEBSITE www.sebastians.com

OPEN	All year
DESCRIPTION	A 1949 host home with views of Hearst Castle and San Simeon Bay.
NO. OF ROOMS	Three rooms share one-and-a-half bathrooms.
RATES	Year-round rates are $99-165 for a single or double. Cancellation requires seven days' notice.
BREAKFAST	Full breakfast is served at Sebastian's patio café.
AMENITIES	Jacuzzi on the garden patio, living room with fireplace.

SANTA BARBARA

The stunning whitewashed buildings, red-tiled roofs, and splendid missions bear witness to Santa Barbara's Spanish influence. The annual Old Days Fiesta in August is a fun way to pay tribute to this legacy. Visit the historic pueblo in downtown Santa Barbara, which features restored 1700s-era structures. Other points of interest include the National History Museum, Botanical Gardens, the Santa Monica Pier, and the Third Street Promenade. Of course, Santa Barbara also boasts beautiful beaches and a spectacular coastline. On clear days, you can see the Channel Islands.

BATH STREET INN

1720 Bath Street, Santa Barbara, CA 93101   805-682-9680
Susan Brown, Innkeeper   800-341-2284
EMAIL bathstin@silicom.com   FAX 805-569-9351
WEBSITE www.silcom.com/~bathstin

OPEN	All year

DESCRIPTION	A 19th-century two-story Queen Anne Victorian inn and adjacent Summer House.
NO. OF ROOMS	Eight rooms in the main house and four rooms in the Summer House with private bathrooms.
RATES	Year-round weekend rates are $105-195 for a single or double. Midweek rates are 20 percent less, except on holidays and during the summer. There is a two-night minimum stay when a Saturday is included.
CREDIT CARDS	American Express, MasterCard, Visa
BREAKFAST	Full breakfast is served in the dining room or in the garden and includes fresh fruit, homemade granola, and a main entrée such as English scones with cheese, frittata, or blueberry pancakes.
AMENITIES	Afternoon tea, evening wine, one room is handicapped accessible.
RESTRICTIONS	No smoking, no pets
MEMBER	Professional Association of Innkeepers International

BLUE DOLPHIN INN

420 W Montecito Street, Santa Barbara, CA 93101   805-965-2333
Pete Chiarenzia & Ed Skolak, Innkeepers   877-722-3657
Spanish and French spoken   FAX 805-962-4907
EMAIL *Info@sbbluedolphininn*   WEBSITE *www.sbbluedolphininn.com*

OPEN	All year
DESCRIPTION	A 1920 Victorian inn furnished with antiques and elegant decor, only 2 blocks from the beach.
NO. OF ROOMS	Nine rooms with private bathrooms.
RATES	Year-round weekend rates are $125-225 for a single or double. There is a two-night minimum stay on weekends, and cancellation requires seven days' notice.
CREDIT CARDS	American Express, MasterCard, Visa
BREAKFAST	Continental plus is served in the dining room. Vegetarian, lowfat, restricted, and other special dietary needs can be accommodated.
AMENITIES	Some rooms with fireplaces and Jacuzzis; wine and cheese; evening dessert; handicapped accessible; king- and queen-size beds.
RESTRICTIONS	No smoking, no pets

Casa del Mar

18 Bath Street, Santa Barbara, CA 93101   805-963-4418
Yum & Yessy Kim, Innkeepers   800-433-3097
Spanish spoken   *FAX 805-966-4240*
EMAIL casadelmar@silicom.com   *WEBSITE www.casadelmar.com*

OPEN	All year
DESCRIPTION	A Mediterranean-style inn built around a garden courtyard, situated less than a block from the beach.
NO. OF ROOMS	Twenty-one rooms and suites with private bathrooms.
RATES	Year-round rates are $69-239 for a single or double. Cancellation requires 48 hours' notice.
CREDIT CARDS	American Express, Diners Club, Discover, MasterCard, Visa
BREAKFAST	Full breakfast is served buffet style.
AMENITIES	Hair dryers, coffee-makers, TV, king- or queen-size beds, whirlpool spa, fax, data ports, fresh flowers, evening wine and cheese.
RESTRICTIONS	No smoking, pets allowed with a $10 fee.

Cheshire Cat Inn

36 W Valerio Street, Santa Barbara, CA 93101   805-569-1610
EMAIL cheshire@cheshirecat.com   *FAX 805-682-1876*
WEBSITE www.cheshirecat.com

OPEN	All year
DESCRIPTION	A two-story Victorian inn decorated with English antiques and Laura Ashley furnishings, surrounded by gardens. There is also a separate cottage.
NO. OF ROOMS	Seventeen rooms, suites, and a cottage with private bathrooms.
RATES	Please inquire about current rates. Business rates are available during midweek. There is a two-night minimum stay during weekends, and cancellation requires seven days' notice with a $15 fee.
BREAKFAST	Full gourmet breakfast is served.
AMENITIES	Fresh flowers; queen- and king-size beds; some rooms have Jacuzzis, fireplaces, refrigerators, and/or balconies; outdoor hot tubs; private decks; afternoon refreshments; evening wine and hors d'oeuvres; off-street parking.
RESTRICTIONS	No smoking inside. Children are welcome in the cottage only.

COAST VILLAGE INN

Santa Barbara, CA	*805-969-3266*
EMAIL *info@coastvillageinn.com*	*800-257-5131 (reservations)*
WEBSITE *www.coastvillageinn.com*	

LOCATION	Three blocks from the beach off Highway 101.
OPEN	All year
NO. OF ROOMS	Twenty-six rooms and suites with private bathrooms.
RATES	Please inquire about current rates. Cancellation requires 48 hours' notice.
CREDIT CARDS	American Express, Discover, MasterCard, Visa
BREAKFAST	Continental breakfast is served at the on-site restaurant.
AMENITIES	Some rooms with ocean views, full kitchens, and/or wet bars; cable TV; ceiling fans; heated pool.

COUNTRY INN BY THE SEA

128 Castillo Street, Santa Barbara, CA 93101	*805-963-4471*
EMAIL *Concierge@innsbythesea.com*	*800-455-4647*
WEBSITE *countryinnbythesea.com*	FAX *805-962-2633*

LOCATION	From the north: Exit Highway 101 at Castillo Street. Turn right on Castillo and drive 2 blocks. From the south: Exit (left lane) at Cabrillo Boulevard. Drive 2.5 miles along the ocean, then turn right onto Castillo Street.
OPEN	All year
DESCRIPTION	A three-story French chateau decorated with luxurious, old-world decor, located one-and-a-half blocks from the beach.
NO. OF ROOMS	Forty-six rooms with private bathrooms.
RATES	Year-round rates are $109-219 for a single or double. There is a two-night minimum stay on weekends, and cancellation requires 72 hours' notice.
CREDIT CARDS	American Express, Discover, MasterCard, Visa
BREAKFAST	Continental plus is served in the dining room and includes muffins, bagels, croissants, pastries, fresh-baked biscuits, jams, cream cheese, assorted juices, fresh fruit, and beverages.
AMENITIES	All rooms have refrigerators, VCRs, irons and ironing boards, libraries; canopy beds; private balconies; fresh-baked cookies; extensive video library.

RESTRICTIONS   No smoking, no pets

RATED   AAA 3 Diamonds

THE EAGLE INN

232 Natoma Avenue, Santa Barbara, CA 93101   805-965-3586
EMAIL *info@theeagleinn.com*   800-767-0030 *(reservations)*
WEBSITE *www.theeagleinn.com/*   FAX 805-966-1218

LOCATION	Between Stearns Wharf and the yacht harbor, 1 block from the beach.
OPEN	All year
DESCRIPTION	A restored Spanish colonial inn with period furnishings.
NO. OF ROOMS	Twenty-seven rooms with private bathrooms.
RATES	Please inquire about current rates and cancellation information.
BREAKFAST	Continental breakfast is served.
AMENITIES	Rooms have cable TV, microwaves, data ports, telephones, hair dryers, coffee-makers; free parking; some rooms have full kitchens.

FRANCISCAN INN

109 Bath Street, Santa Barbara, CA 93101   805-963-8845
Debbie Neer, Innkeeper   FAX 805-564-3295
Spanish and some Japanese spoken
WEBSITE *www.franciscaninn.com*

LOCATION	Take Cabrillo Boulevard west along the beach. Turn right onto Bath Street.
OPEN	All year
DESCRIPTION	A 1925 Spanish inn and a 1976 Mediterranean inn with country and waverly decor, situated 1 block from the beach and harbor.
NO. OF ROOMS	Fifty-three rooms with private bathrooms.
RATES	May 15 through September, rates are $85-115 for a single or double and $115-195 for a suite. October through May 14, rates are $65-115 for a single or double and $115-175 for a suite. There is a minimum stay on some weekends, and cancellation requires 48 hours' notice.
CREDIT CARDS	American Express, Carte Blanche, Diners Club, Discover, En Route, MasterCard, Visa

BREAKFAST	Continental breakfast is served in the lobby and includes fresh-baked muffins, bagels, croissants, orange juice, fresh fruit, coffee, cocoa, spiced cider, and tea.
AMENITIES	Heated pool; Jacuzzi; 24-hour coffee, tea, cocoa, spiced cider; in-room VCR with free video library; library in lobby; free parking; afternoon reception with hot homemade cookies, beverages, and fruit.
RESTRICTIONS	None
REVIEWED	*Frommer's, Romantic Santa Barbara*
RATED	AAA 3 Diamonds, Mobil 3 Stars

GLENBOROUGH INN

1327 Bath Street, Santa Barbara, CA 93101   805-966-0589
Michael & Steve, Innkeepers   800-962-0589
Spanish spoken   FAX 805-564-8610
EMAIL *glenboro@silcom.com*   WEBSITE *www.silcom.com/~glenboro*

LOCATION	Take Highway 101 to the Carrillo Street exit. Head east on Carrillo toward "downtown" Santa Barbara, and turn left onto Bath Street.
OPEN	All year
DESCRIPTION	Two 1885 two-story Victorian and California Craftsman inns with gardens and outdoor sitting areas, located in a historic downtown residential area.
NO. OF ROOMS	Fourteen rooms with private bathrooms. Try the Riviera Suite.
RATES	Year-round rates are $100-360 for a single or double, $210-360 for a suite, and $360 for the guesthouse. There is a minimum stay during weekends. Inquire about a cancellation policy.
CREDIT CARDS	American Express, Diners Club, Discover, MasterCard, Visa
BREAKFAST	Full breakfast is served in the guestrooms and includes fruit smoothie, fresh fruit bowl, baked breads, and an entrée.
AMENITIES	Flowers, luxurious robes, private garden hot tub, social hour, garden sitting areas, garden swing.
RESTRICTIONS	No smoking, no pets
REVIEWED	*Fodor's; Country Inns and Backroads; Southern California: Off the Beaten Path; Best Places to Stay in California; Hidden Coast of California; Recommended Country Inns: West Coast*
MEMBER	Professional Association of Innkeepers International, California Lodging Industry Association, California Association of Bed & Breakfast Inns
RATED	AAA 2 Diamonds, Mobil 2 Stars

HARBOR HOUSE INN

104 Bath Street, Santa Barbara, CA 93101	*805-962-9745*
Judy Marr, Innkeeper	*888-474-6789*
EMAIL *judy@harborhouseinn.com*	WEBSITE *harborhouseinn.com*

LOCATION	Exit Highway 101 at Cabrillo Boulevard. Turn left toward the ocean and go about 1.5 miles until you pass the pier (at the end of State Street). Drive 2 blocks west of the pier and turn right on Bath Street.
OPEN	All year
DESCRIPTION	A 1948 one-story California adobe inn decorated with many fine antiques, located near the beach.
NO. OF ROOMS	Ten rooms with private bathrooms.
RATES	June through August, rates are $78-108 for a single or double and $88-138 for a suite. September through May, rates are $68-98 for a single or double and $78-118 for a suite. There is a minimum stay when a Saturday is involved, and cancellation requires 48 hours' notice.
CREDIT CARDS	American Express, Diners Club, Discover, MasterCard, Visa
BREAKFAST	Continental plus is served in the dining room and includes homemade bread and muffins, fruit, juice, cereal, coffee, tea, and assorted treats.
AMENITIES	Bicycles available; most suites have kitchens; some have separate living rooms.
RESTRICTIONS	No smoking. Shorty and Muffin are the resident pooches.

INN ON SUMMER HILL

2520 Lillie Avenue, Summerland, CA 93067	*805-969-9998*
Paul & Mabel Shults, Innkeepers	*800-845-5566*
EMAIL *denisel@innonsummerhill.com*	FAX *805-565-9946*
WEBSITE *www.innonsummerhill.com*	

LOCATION	Six miles south of Santa Barbara in the seaside village of Summerland, on the north side of Highway 101.
OPEN	All year
DESCRIPTION	A 1989 two-story California Craftsman inn with English country decor.
NO. OF ROOMS	Sixteen rooms with private bathrooms.

RATES	Year-round rates are $215-325 for a single or double. Additional guests are $25 per person. There is a two-night minimum stay during weekends and holidays, and cancellation requires seven days' notice.
CREDIT CARDS	American Express, Discover, MasterCard, Visa
BREAKFAST	Full gourmet breakfast is served in the Teapot Room or guestrooms and includes breads, pastries, cereals, seasonal fruit, a hot entrée, fresh-squeezed juices, and a selection of teas and coffee.
AMENITIES	All rooms have ocean views with balconies or patios; fireplaces; TV/VCR; stereo; mini-refrigerators; robes; whirlpool tubs; fresh flowers in all rooms; afternoon refreshments and desserts; packages available.
RESTRICTIONS	No smoking, no pets
REVIEWED	*Country Inns* magazine, *Country Accents* magazine, *Travel & Leisure* magazine, *The Best Places to Kiss in Southern California*, *Brides* magazine
MEMBER	California Association of Bed & Breakfast Inns, Professional Association of Innkeepers International
RATED	AAA 4 Diamonds, ABBA 4 Crowns, Best Places to Kiss 3 Lips, Mobil 3 Stars

IVANHOE INN

1406 Castillo Street, Santa Barbara, CA 93101   805-963-8832

MARY MAY INN

111 W Valerio Street, Santa Barbara, CA 93101   805-569-3398
WEBSITE *www.marymayinn.com*

OPEN	All year
DESCRIPTION	Two elegantly restored 1800s-era buildings with period decor.
NO. OF ROOMS	Twelve rooms with private bathrooms.
RATES	Please inquire about current rates and discounts.
BREAKFAST	Continental breakfast is served.
AMENITIES	Evening tea; all rooms have queen-size beds; some rooms have canopy beds, Jacuzzi tubs, and/or wood-burning fireplaces.

MONTECITO INN

1295 Coast Village Road, Montecito, CA 93108	805-969-7854

1295 Coast Village Road, Montecito, CA 93108   805-969-7854
EMAIL info@montecitoinn.com   800-843-2017
WEBSITE www.montecitoinn.com   *FAX 805-969-0623*

LOCATION	Four miles east of downtown Santa Barbara, 2 blocks from the beach.
OPEN	All year
DESCRIPTION	An elegant 1928 three-story Spanish-style hotel with Italian marble floors in the lobby and French provincial decor. The inn was built by Charlie Chaplin.
NO. OF ROOMS	Sixty rooms and suites with private bathrooms.
RATES	Please inquire about current rates. Cancellation requires 48 hours' notice.
CREDIT CARDS	American Express, Discover, MasterCard, Visa
BREAKFAST	Continental breakfast is served in the on-site café. Lunch and dinner are also available.
AMENITIES	Fresh flowers; fireplace in lobby; pool; hot tub; sauna; conference facility; complete library of Charlie Chaplin films; handpainted tiles in bathrooms; armoires; ceiling fans; cable TV/VCRs; room service; luxury suites feature marble bathrooms, Jacuzzi tubs, and fireplaces; complimentary trolley passes; bikes; free parking.

MOUNTAIN VIEW INN

3055 De La Vina Street, Santa Barbara, CA 93105   805-687-6636

OLD YACHT CLUB INN

431 Corona Del Mar Drive, Santa Barbara, CA 93103   805-962-1277
Nancy Donaldson & Sandy Hunt, Innkeepers   800-676-1676
Spanish and German spoken   *FAX 805-962-3989*
EMAIL oyci@aol.com

LOCATION	Take Highway 101 to Cabrillo Boulevard (exits left), go west approximately 1 mile to Corona del Mar Drive, and turn right.
OPEN	All year

DESCRIPTION	Two California Craftsman and early California-style buildings, constructed in 1912 and 1925, with turn-of-the-century decor.
NO. OF ROOMS	Twelve rooms with private bathrooms. Try the Santa Rosa Suite.
RATES	Rates are $105-185 for a single or double and $185 for a suite. Midweek rates from October through May are $90-165 for a single or double and $165 for a suite. There is a two-night minimum stay if a Saturday night is involved, and cancellation requires one week's notice.
CREDIT CARDS	American Express, Discover, MasterCard, Visa
BREAKFAST	Full breakfast is served in the dining room and includes fresh juice and fruit, omelets, home-baked breads, French toast, pancakes, or a baked egg dish. Dinner is available on Saturday evenings only.
AMENITIES	Complimentary evening wine, bicycles, beach chairs, towels, fresh flowers and carafe of sherry in each room, telephones, fax, Internet access.
RESTRICTIONS	No smoking, no pets
REVIEWED	*The Best Places to Stay in California, Recommended Inns of the West Coast, The Best Places to Kiss in Southern California, Fodor's California*
MEMBER	Bed & Breakfast Innkeepers of California, Professional Association of Innkeepers International
RATED	AAA 2 Diamonds, Mobil 2 Stars
AWARDS	1993, 10 Best Inns, Uncle Ben's; 1993, 10 Best Inns, *Bon Appetit*

OLIVE HOUSE BED & BREAKFAST

1604 Olive Street, Santa Barbara, CA 93101   *805-962-4902*
Ellen Schaub, Innkeeper   *800-786-6422*
EMAIL olivehse@aol.com   *FAX 805-962-9983*
WEBSITE www.sbinns.com/oliveinn

LOCATION	Take Highway 101 to the State Street exit. Turn right on Arrellaga, then left onto Olive Street.
OPEN	All year
DESCRIPTION	A 1906 two-story California Craftsman inn with exposed redwood beams, window seats, and stained-glass windows.
NO. OF ROOMS	Six rooms with private bathrooms. Try the Bella Vista Room.
RATES	May through December, rates are $110-180 for a single or double. January through April there is a 20 percent discount during midweek. There is a two-night minimum stay on weekends, and cancellation requires seven days' notice.

Olive House Bed & Breakfast, Santa Barbara

CREDIT CARDS	American Express, Discover, MasterCard, Visa
BREAKFAST	Full breakfast is served and includes quiche, French toast, juice, fruit, tea, and coffee.
AMENITIES	Coffee, tea, and cookies always available; wine and cheese in the evening; sherry available for nightcaps; private hot tubs; fireplace in the living room.
RESTRICTIONS	No smoking, no pets, children over 14 are welcome. Felix, Trixie, and Toni are the resident cats.
REVIEWED	*The Best Places to Kiss in Southern California; The Official Guide to American Historic Inns; The National Trust Guide to Historic Bed & Breakfasts, Inns, and Small Hotels; Away for the Weekend; Non-Smokers Guide to Bed & Breakfasts*

PARSONAGE BED & BREAKFAST INN

1600 Olive Street, Santa Barbara, CA 93101   805-962-9336
EMAIL info@parsonage.com   800-775-0532
WEBSITE www.parsonage.com   FAX 805-962-2285

LOCATION	Close to downtown Santa Barbara and the beach.
OPEN	All year
DESCRIPTION	A restored 1892 two-story Queen Anne Victorian inn with period decor and antiques.
NO. OF ROOMS	Six rooms with private bathrooms.
RATES	Please inquire about current rates. There is a two-night minimum stay when a Saturday night is involved, three nights during some holidays; cancellation requires seven days' notice.
CREDIT CARDS	American Express, Discover, MasterCard, Visa
BREAKFAST	Full gourmet breakfast is served.
AMENITIES	Hors d'oeuvres; robes; the honeymoon suite has a Jacuzzi for two, king-size bed, views of the ocean and city; two rooms have fireplaces.
RESTRICTIONS	No smoking inside, no pets
RATED	AAA 3 Diamond

SECRET GARDEN INN & COTTAGES

1908 Bath Street, Santa Barbara, CA 93101   805-687-2300
Jack Greenwald & Christine Dunstan, Innkeepers   800-676-1622
EMAIL garden@secretgarden.com   FAX 805-687-4576
WEBSITE www.secretgarden.com

LOCATION	Eight blocks from downtown Santa Barbara.
OPEN	All year
DESCRIPTION	A renovated 1905 inn and five Craftsman cottages, decorated with Early American antiques, wicker furniture, and quilts.

NO. OF ROOMS	Eleven rooms with private bathrooms.
RATES	Year-round rates are $110-195 for a single or double. There is a two-night minimum stay when a Saturday is included, and cancellation requires seven days' notice.
CREDIT CARDS	American Express, Discover, MasterCard, Visa
BREAKFAST	Full California breakfast is served in the dining room, on the cottage patios, or under the trees in the garden and includes fresh fruit, homemade coffeecakes, scones, and an egg specialty.
AMENITIES	Hot tubs, massage, privacy.
RESTRICTIONS	No smoking indoors, no pets, children are welcome.

SIMPSON HOUSE INN

121 E Arrellaga, Santa Barbara, CA 93101   805-963-7067
Glyn & Linda Sue Davies, Innkeepers   800-676-1280
French and Spanish spoken   FAX 805-564-4811
EMAIL *reservations@simpsonhouseinn.com*
WEBSITE *www.simpsonhouseinn.com*

LOCATION	From Highway 101 north, take the Garden Street exit, turn left at the first signal, then right onto Garden Street. Drive 17 blocks and turn left onto East Arrellaga.
OPEN	All year
DESCRIPTION	An 1874 two-story Italianate Victorian inn with period decor, secluded on an acre of English gardens.
NO. OF ROOMS	Fourteen rooms with private bathrooms.
RATES	Year-round rates are $175 for a single or double. There is a two-night minimum stay when a Saturday is involved, and cancellation requires seven days' notice.
CREDIT CARDS	American Express, Discover, MasterCard, Visa
BREAKFAST	Full gourmet breakfast is served in the dining room, on the veranda, or on the garden patios and includes fresh juice, homemade granola, seasonal fruit, and an entrée such as fresh strawberry crepes, plus fresh-brewed coffee and a large selection of English or herbal teas.
AMENITIES	Evening Mediterranean hors d'oeuvres buffet, local wine, afternoon tea and cookies, robes, truffles with turndown service, full concierge service, bicycles, croquet.
RESTRICTIONS	No smoking, no pets, children over 12 are welcome. Children and extra-person occupancies are restricted to specific rooms and limited to certain days of the week. Bella and Mia are the resident black Labs.

REVIEWED	*The Official Guide to American Historic Inns*
MEMBER	Independent Innkeepers of America, California Association of Bed & Breakfast Inns
RATED	AAA 5 Diamonds, ABBA 4 Crowns, Mobil 4 Stars
AWARDS	The only B&B in North America to receive a 5-Diamond rating from AAA
KUDOS/COMMENTS	"The B&B of B&Bs. What you think a B&B should be. First class." "Lovely, formal inn."

STATE STREET HOTEL

121 State Street, Santa Barbara, CA 93101   *805-966-6586*

SUMMERLAND INN

2161 Ortega Hill Road, Summerland, CA 93067   *805-969-5225*
Terry Hougan, Innkeeper   *800-746-7930*
Spanish and Japanese spoken   *FAX 805-565-0389*
WEBSITE www.summerland-inn.com

LOCATION	Within easy walking distance of Summerland Beach.
OPEN	All year
NO. OF ROOMS	Twelve rooms with private bathrooms.
RATES	High-season rates are $99-170 for a single or double. Off-season rates are $69-160. There is a two-night minimum stay on weekends, and cancellation requires 72 hours' notice.
CREDIT CARDS	American Express, MasterCard, Visa
BREAKFAST	Full breakfast is served on weekends and continental is served midweek.
AMENITIES	Conference and wedding facilities, afternoon snacks, TV, queen- or king-size beds, fax, data ports.
RESTRICTIONS	No smoking, no pets, children are welcome.

Tiffany Inn

1323 De La Vina Street, Santa Barbara, CA 93101   805-963-2283
Carol & Larry MacDonald, Innkeepers   800-999-5672
EMAIL tiffanyinn@aol.com   FAX 805-962-0994
WEBSITE www.sbinns.com/tiffany

OPEN	All year
DESCRIPTION	A grand 1898 two-story Victorian home, decorated with antiques, located in a quiet residential neighborhood.
NO. OF ROOMS	Five rooms and two suites with private bathrooms.
RATES	Please call for current rates. There is a two-night minimum stay on weekends, three nights on holiday weekends; cancellation requires seven days' notice.
CREDIT CARDS	American Express, MasterCard, Visa
BREAKFAST	Full breakfast is served in the dining room, in guestrooms, or on the veranda and may include the inn's signature dish, orange-filled crepes with raspberry sauce. Special meals available upon request.
AMENITIES	Telephone, queen- and king-size beds, fireplaces, afternoon wine and cheese, handicapped accessible, cookies in the evening.
RESTRICTIONS	No smoking, no pets, accommodations are not suitable for children.
MEMBER	Professional Association of Innkeepers International, California Association of Bed & Breakfast Inns

The Upham Hotel & Garden Cottages

1404 De La Vina Street, Santa Barbara, CA 93101   805-962-0058
Jan Martin Winn, Innkeeper   800-727-0876
Spanish spoken   FAX 805-963-2825
WEBSITE www.californiainns.com

LOCATION	From Highway 101 north, take the Arrellaga exit. At the off-ramp, go straight about 2 blocks, make a right onto De La Vina Street, and drive one-and-a-half blocks. From Highway 101 south, take the Mission exit, turn left at the off-ramp, and right at De La Vina.
OPEN	All year
DESCRIPTION	An 1871 Italianate hotel and California Craftsman cottages decorated with classic Victorian furnishings, situated on an acre of gardens.

The Upham Hotel & Garden Cottages, Santa Barbara

NO. OF ROOMS	Fifty rooms with private bathrooms. Jan recommends the Master Suite with the Jacuzzi tub.
RATES	Year-round rates are $145-385 for a single or double and $245-385 for a suite. There is a two-night minimum stay on weekends, and cancellation requires three days' notice.
CREDIT CARDS	American Express, Carte Blanche, Diners Club, Discover, MasterCard, Visa
BREAKFAST	Continental breakfast is served in the lobby of the main building and includes coffee, tea, juices, an assortment of croissants, bagels, scones, pastries, cinnamon rolls, pecan rolls, muffins, and hot and cold cereals.
AMENITIES	Afternoon wine and cheese; bedtime Oreo cookies and milk; morning paper; on-site restaurant; meeting and banquet facilities; some rooms with gas fireplaces, private patios, porches.
RESTRICTIONS	No pets. Henry is the resident cat.
REVIEWED	*Frommer's, The Official Guide to American Historic Inns, Destinations of Southern California, Elegant Small Hotels, The Best Places to Kiss in Southern California, Country Inns of California, Romantic Southern California*
MEMBER	California Association of Bed & Breakfast Inns

VILLA D'ITALIA

Santa Barbara, CA   805-687-6933

VILLA ROSA INN

15 Chapala Street, Santa Barbara, CA 93111   805-966-0851
Annie Puetz, Innkeeper   FAX 805-962-7159
Spanish, Flemish, French, Dutch, and some German spoken

LOCATION
From the north, take Highway 101 south to Castillo Street. Turn right at the stoplight and follow Castillo Street to Cabrillo Boulevard. Turn left at the stoplight, follow Cabrillo Boulevard to Chapala Street, and turn left.

OPEN
All year

DESCRIPTION
A renovated 1930 two-story hacienda-style inn with Spanish-influenced furnishings, neutral tones, exposed wood, and a private, plant-filled courtyard.

NO. OF ROOMS
Eighteen rooms with private bathrooms.

RATES
July through September, rates are $110-200 for a single or double and $230 for a deluxe room. October through June, rates are $100-190 for a single or double and $200-205 for a deluxe room. There is a minimum stay on weekends and holidays, and cancellation requires five days' notice.

CREDIT CARDS
American Express, MasterCard, Visa

BREAKFAST
Continental breakfast is served in the lobby and includes bagels, assorted pastries, muffins, croissants, orange juice, coffee, assorted teas, and hot chocolate.

AMENITIES
Evening wine and hors d'oeuvres, nightcap of port or sherry, evening turndown service with rose and chocolates, robes, hair dryers.

RESTRICTIONS
No smoking, no pets, children over 14 are welcome.

SANTA MONICA

With its broad, white beaches, bustling promenade, and restored historic pier, Santa Monica is becoming a major tourist area. It is also the gateway to the Santa Monica Mountains National Recreation Area, a 50-mile-long botanical island. Beverly Hills is a few miles to the northeast.

CHANNEL ROAD INN

219 West Channel Road, Santa Monica, CA 90402   310-459-1920
Susan Zolla, Innkeeper   FAX 310-454-9920
Spanish and Italian spoken
EMAIL *Channelinn@aol.com*
WEBSITE *www.channelroadinn.com*

LOCATION	Take Highway 10 west until it ends at Pacific Coast Highway north. Take Pacific Coast Highway north 1.8 miles to the stoplight for West Channel Road and make a hard right.
OPEN	All year
DESCRIPTION	A 1910 three-story shingle-clad colonial revival with seashore, antiques, and country decor, located 1 block from the beach in rustic Santa Monica Canyon.
NO. OF ROOMS	Fourteen rooms with private bathrooms.
RATES	Year-round rates are $145-245 for a single or double and $255-295 for a suite. There is no minimum stay, and cancellation requires 72 hours' notice.
CREDIT CARDS	American Express, MasterCard, Visa
BREAKFAST	Full breakfast is served in the dining room and includes apple French toast, raisin scones, fresh fruit, granola, coffee, tea, and fresh juice.
AMENITIES	Afternoon tea and cookies, evening wine and cheese, thick robes, hot tub in garden, bicycles.
RESTRICTIONS	No smoking inside
REVIEWED	*The Best Places to Kiss in Southern California, Access LA, Fodor's, Karen Brown's California: Charming Inns & Itineraries*
MEMBER	Professional Association of Innkeepers International, California Association of Bed & Breakfast Inns
RATED	AAA 3 Diamonds, ABBA 4 Crowns, Mobil 3 Stars
AWARDS	1998, Certificate of Commendation, Los Angeles City Council; 1990, Best New Business, Pacific Palisades Chamber of Commerce

SANTA PAULA

Santa Paula holds dual distinctions. It is both the Citrus Capital of the World and the Antique Airplane Capital of the World. The Unocal Union Oil Museum is an interesting stop. Lakes Piru and Casitas, state beaches, and National Forest lands are all close at hand. Santa Paula is a dozen miles east of Ventura on scenic Highway 126.

THE FERN OAKS INN

1025 Ojai Road, Santa Paula, CA 93060   805-525-7747
Anthony & Marcia Landau, Innkeepers   FAX 805-933-5001
French, Spanish, and Farsi spoken
EMAIL info@fernoaksinn.com
WEBSITE www.fernoaksinn.com

LOCATION	Sixty-five miles northwest of Los Angeles and 14 miles east of the city of Ventura and the Pacific Ocean.
OPEN	All year
DESCRIPTION	A 1929 Spanish revival inn with hardwood floors, faux-finish painted walls with Bacheldor fireplace, antique furnishings, a piano, and Tiffany lamps representing the 1930s era, situated on a 0.75-acre property with rose gardens and fruit trees.
NO. OF ROOMS	Four rooms with private bathrooms. Try the Casablanca Room.
RATES	Rates are year round. There is a minimum stay during holidays. Cancellation requires 72 hours' notice and a $15 charge.
CREDIT CARDS	No
BREAKFAST	Full gourmet breakfast is served in the dining room or outside on the patio/yard and includes fruit salad, New Orleans caramelized French toast, fresh orange juice, coffee, tea, homemade cookies, and pastries.
AMENITIES	Complimentary imported sherry, port, and wine; afternoon tea and pastries; flowers and chocolate in each bedroom; meeting facility; large pool; air conditioning; hiking trail.
RESTRICTIONS	Smoking outside only, children on a limited basis. Layla is the resident cat. Amrosia is the parrot. "We also have a semi-independent chicken named Tree Topper who, unlike the rest of the chickens in the backyard, likes to sleep separately and alone on the top of the orange tree."

SOLVANG

A bit of Denmark in the beautiful Santa Ynez Valley, Solvang was founded by Danes back in 1911. Windmills still mark the landscape and horse-drawn streetcars, called "Honen," continue to cart tourists through town. The local pastries are sinfully delicious. Stop by for a few during Danish Days in September. In the summer, take in the performances at Theaterfest, held in the 800-seat outdoor theater. From Santa Barbara, Solvang is 45 miles northwest via Highways 101 and 246.

CHIMNEY SWEEP INN

1564 Copenhagen Drive, Solvang, CA 93463   805-688-2111

PETERSEN VILLAGE INN

1576 Mission Drive, Solvang, CA 93463   805-688-3121
WEBSITE www.peterseninn.com   800-321-8985

STORYBOOK INN BED & BREAKFAST

409 1st Street, Solvang, CA 93463   805-688-1703
The Orton Family, Innkeepers   800-786-7925
WEBSITE www.bbchannel.com/bbc/p213661.asp   FAX 805-688-0953

OPEN	All year
DESCRIPTION	A three-story European-style villa decorated with antiques and paintings by a local artist.
NO. OF ROOMS	Nine rooms with private bathrooms.
RATES	Please inquire about current rates and cancellation information.
CREDIT CARDS	American Express, Discover, MasterCard, Visa
BREAKFAST	Full breakfast is served on weekends. Continental is served midweek and includes fresh fruit, pastries, and Danish specialties.
AMENITIES	Queen-size beds, marble fireplaces, on-site restaurant.
RESTRICTIONS	No pets, no smoking, the inn is not suitable for children.
MEMBER	California Association of Bed & Breakfast Inns

SPRINGVILLE

Springville was originally noted for its Soda Springs. Today the main draws are Sequoia National Forest and, just to the north, Sequoia National Park. Springville is also handy to Lake Success and is situated just above the Tule River Indian Reservation. Check out the Jackass Mail Run during the third weekend in April, the Springville Rodeo over the last weekend in April, and the popular Apple Festival during the third weekend in October. Springville is east of Highway 99 on Highway 190.

ANNIE'S BED & BREAKFAST

33024 Globe Drive, Springville, CA 93265   559-539-3827
Ann & John Bozanich, Innkeepers   FAX 559-539-2179
Sign language
EMAIL *bozanich@lightspeed.net*
WEBSITE *www.bbchannel.com/bbc/p213608.asp*

OPEN	All year
DESCRIPTION	A country inn furnished with antiques and handmade quilts, situated on 5 acres in the foothills of the Sierra Mountains.
NO. OF ROOMS	Three rooms with private bathrooms.
RATES	Please inquire about current rates and cancellation information.
CREDIT CARDS	American Express, Diners Club, Discover, MasterCard, Visa
BREAKFAST	Full country breakfast is prepared on an antique wood-burning cookstove.
AMENITIES	Pool; spa; piano; stocked guest refrigerator; coffee-maker; evening dessert, cordials, hors d'oeuvres; handicapped accessible.
RESTRICTIONS	No smoking, no pets, the B&B is not suitable for children.
MEMBER	California Association of Bed & Breakfast Inns, Professional Association of Innkeepers International

MOUNTAIN TOP BED & BREAKFAST

56816 Aspen Drive, Springville, CA 93265   559-542-2639

THE SPRINGVILLE INN

35634 Highway 190, Springville, CA 93265   559-539-2611
Carleen M. Kemmerling, Innkeeper   800-484-3466
EMAIL *CarMKem@aol.com*   FAX 559-539-7502
WEBSITE *www.springvilleinn.com*

LOCATION	North of Bakersfield, south of Fresno and Visalia, and east of Porterville, in the foothills of the Sierra Nevada. The inn is situated in the exact center of town "and practically makes up the town. You cannot miss us—we have a red stagecoach perched on the roof of the inn."
OPEN	All year
DESCRIPTION	A remodeled 1911 two-and-a-half-story western-style inn decorated with antiques and country charm.
NO. OF ROOMS	Eleven rooms with private bathrooms.
RATES	April through December, rates are $75-95 for a single or double. January through March, rates are $55-75 for a single or double. There is a minimum stay during major events, and cancellation requires 48 hours' notice, seven days during major events.
CREDIT CARDS	American Express, Diners Club, Discover, MasterCard, Visa
BREAKFAST	Country continental breakfast is served in the dining room or guestrooms and includes quiche, sweet rolls or coffeecake, fresh fruit, orange juice, coffee, and tea. Lunch and dinner are also available.
AMENITIES	Small fruit basket on arrival; full-service restaurant and bar; banquet facilities (with kitchen, full bar, dance floor, bandstand, outside patio); outside patio for dining; bathroom toiletries; air conditioning, ceiling fan, cable TV, telephone in every room.
RESTRICTIONS	None. Horses and cattle roam the hills all around the inn. Owners sometimes bring their dogs to the inn.
MEMBER	Sequoia Bed & Breakfast Association, California Association of Bed & Breakfast Inns

SUGAR PINE

COUNTRY INN AT SUGAR PINE
BED & BREAKFAST

19958 Middle Camp–Sugar Pine Road,   209-586-4615
Sugar Pine, CA 95346   800-292-2093
Nancy Mulkey, Innkeeper

SUNSET BEACH

HARBOUR INN AT SUNSET BEACH

16912 Pacific Coast Highway, Sunset Beach, CA 90742   562-592-4770

TEMECULA

A prime grape-growing region of the Temecula Valley, there are over a dozen wineries close at hand, all offering tours and tastings. The annual Balloon and Wine Festival in May is a major event. Downtown's Old West Main Street is worth exploring, and Lake Skinner Recreation Area offers great fishing and swimming. Temecula is within an hour's drive of both Los Angeles and San Diego, halfway between Riverside and San Diego on I-15.

LOMA VISTA BED & BREAKFAST

33350 La Serena Way, Temecula, CA 92591   909-676-7047

PIERSON'S COUNTRY PLACE

25185 Pierson Road, Homeland, CA 92548   909-926-4546
Kay & Mike Pierson, Innkeepers   FAX 909-926-1456
EMAIL piersonscountryplace@linkline.com
WEBSITE www.linkline.com/personal/piersonscountryplace

LOCATION	From the junction of I-215 and Highway 74 east, travel east 3 miles (past three traffic lights) to Sultanus and turn left. Drive about 0.5 mile to Watson (the second street) and turn right. Drive about 0.25 mile to Pierson Road (second street) and turn left. Go past Alicante Street to two white columns and a wrought-iron gate. Ring the bell.
OPEN	All year
DESCRIPTION	A 1996 two-story Mediterranean-style inn with an open, light, spacious decor, located on 5 gated acres overlooking the valley. The circular drive is lined with roses and gazanias and leads to a front lawn surrounded by trees.
NO. OF ROOMS	Five rooms with private bathrooms.
RATES	Year-round weekend and holiday rates are $125 for a single or double. Midweek rates are $100. There is no minimum stay, and cancellation requires five days' notice.
CREDIT CARDS	MasterCard, Visa
BREAKFAST	Full breakfast is served in the dining room and includes coffee, tea, fresh orange juice, fresh-baked blueberry muffins, cantaloupe and watermelon, shirred eggs with sauce, spicy sausage patty, French toast with maple syrup, fresh-baked biscuits, and specialty gravy.
AMENITIES	Vase of freshly cut flowers; candy dish; spa in secluded setting; each room has air conditioning and an overhead fan; hors d'oeuvres with wine, beer, or fruit juices served evenings; two rooms are handicapped accessible.
RESTRICTIONS	Smoking allowed at spa area only, no pets, no children. Tracie is the resident Lab; Tammy is the Pomeranian. There are also chickens and ducks on the property.
REVIEWED	*Stash Tea Bed & Breakfast Guide*

TEMPLETON

COUNTRY HOUSE INN

91 South Main Street, Templeton, CA 93465   805-434-1598

THREE RIVERS

On scenic Highway 198, just north of Lake Kaweah, Three Rivers lies on the threshold of Sequoia and Kings Canyon National Parks. Enjoy the Jazz Affair in April and the Redbud Arts and Crafts Festival in May.

CINNAMON CREEK RANCH

PO Box 54, Three Rivers, CA 93271   559-561-1107
EMAIL *cinnamon@theworks.com*
WEBSITE *members.tripod.com/CCreek/index.htm*

LOCATION	From Highway 198 east, drive 18 miles to Three Rivers.
OPEN	All year
DESCRIPTION	A ranch house with country decor, situated on 10 acres in the foothills of the Sierra Mountains along the South Fork of the Kaweah River.
RATES	Please inquire about current rates. Cancellation requires one week's notice.
CREDIT CARDS	MasterCard, Visa
BREAKFAST	Continental breakfast is served.
AMENITIES	Rooms have TV/VCRs, coffee-makers, flowers, bottled water; the cabin has a full kitchen; some rooms are handicapped accessible.
RESTRICTIONS	No smoking, ask about pets, children are welcome.

CORT COTTAGE

PO Box 245, Three Rivers, CA 93271   559-561-4671
Elsah Cort, Innkeeper
EMAIL *elsah@theworks.com*
WEBSITE *www.sequoiabedandbreakfast.com*

LOCATION	Four miles from the entrance to Sequoia National Park at the end of the road in Salt Creek Canyon, 1 mile off Highway 198.
OPEN	All year
DESCRIPTION	A private guesthouse designed by the previous owner/architect with simple, comfortable furnishings and featuring panoramic views of Salt Creek Canyon. The cottage is niched into the hillside and adjacent to the Case Mountain public land area.
NO. OF ROOMS	One room with a private bathroom.

RATES	Year-round rate is $95 for a single or double and $10 for each additional guest. There is a two-night or three-night minimum stay during holiday weekends. A nonrefundable first night's deposit is required.
CREDIT CARDS	MasterCard, Visa
BREAKFAST	Continental plus is available in the kitchen and includes homemade muffins, fresh fruit, homemade granola or other dry cereal, juice, milk, real butter, eggs (which guests prepare themselves), coffee, and teas.
AMENITIES	Hot tub under the stars, TV/VCR, extensive library, fully equipped kitchen, deck with mountain view, air conditioning, robes, iron and ironing board, herb garden.
RESTRICTIONS	No smoking inside, no pets, all children are welcome. Midas, Monkey, and Milly are the resident cats. They are not allowed in the cottage.
REVIEWED	*Bed & Breakfast USA, The California Bed & Breakfast Book, Southern California: Off the Beaten Path*

ORGANIC GARDENS BED & BREAKFAST

44095 Dinely Drive, Three Rivers, CA 93271 559-561-0916
Brenda Stoltzfus & Saundra Sturdevant, Innkeepers FAX 559-561-1017
Chinese, Tagalog, and Japanese spoken
EMAIL *eggplant@theworks.com*
WEBSITE *www.theworks.com/~eggplant*

LOCATION	If coming from Visalia, turn left onto Dinely Drive, then bear right at the Y and drive 0.5 mile.
OPEN	All year
DESCRIPTION	A 1980 two-story natural-wood host home with tiled floors, large windows, and original photographs, situated in the foothills just outside of Sequoia National Park, with panoramic views of the usually snowcapped mountains.
NO. OF ROOMS	Two rooms with private bathrooms.
RATES	Year-round rates are $115-130 for a single or double. There is a two-night minimum stay, and cancellation requires seven days' notice.
CREDIT CARDS	MasterCard, Visa
BREAKFAST	Full vegetarian or vegan breakfast is served outside on the decks. Ingredients are all organic, including coffee and milk.

AMENITIES	Robes, outdoor hot tub with mountain views, air conditioning, cast-iron gas heaters, porch swings, and deck.
RESTRICTIONS	No smoking, no pets, children over five are welcome. There are resident cats.
MEMBER	Sequoia Area Bed & Breakfast Association

TWENTYNINE PALMS

Back in the 1870s, exactly 29 palms bordered this oasis between the Mojave and Colorado Deserts. Today it serves as the northern entrance to Joshua Tree National Park, which features world-class rock climbing. The Mojave National Preserve and Morongo Wildlife Sanctuary are also close at hand. Twentynine Palms is about 40 miles northeast of Palm Springs via Highway 62.

29 PALMS INN

73950 Inn Avenue, Twentynine Palms, CA 92277   760-367-3505
Jane & Paul Smith, Innkeepers   FAX 760-367-4425
Spanish spoken
EMAIL *29palmsinn@eee.org*
WEBSITE *www.29palmsinn.com*

LOCATION	Taking Twentynine Palms Highway (Highway 62) east into town, look for National Park Drive (1 block east of the lighted intersection at Adobe Road), and turn right (south). Go about 0.25 mile down National Park Drive and turn right onto Inn Avenue.
OPEN	All year
DESCRIPTION	Adobe bungalows, wood-frame cabins, a three-bedroom guesthouse, and adobe house with a private fruit-tree patio. The property is adjacent to Joshua Tree National Park on the Oasis of Mara in the Mojave Desert.
NO. OF ROOMS	Nineteen rooms with private bathrooms. Try Irene's Adobe.
RATES	September 16 through June 14, rates are $62-260 for a single or double. June 15 through September 15, rates are $47-230 for a single or double. There is a minimum stay during weekends and holidays, and cancellation requires 48 hours' notice with a $10 charge.
CREDIT CARDS	American Express, Diners Club, Discover, MasterCard, Visa
BREAKFAST	Continental breakfast is served in the dining room and includes coffee, juice, tea, and fresh-baked goodies such as sourdough bread, blueberry muffins, or poppyseed bread. Lunch, dinner, boxed lunches for picnics, and catering are also available.

AMENITIES	Heated pool adjacent to the full-service bar and patio, Swedish massage available for an additional charge, Jacuzzi, library/reading room with many unusual books. "Our restaurant features wonderful lunches and dinners daily, and a champagne brunch on Sundays." (Meals not included in room price.)
RESTRICTIONS	None. Mara is the resident cat, and there are a number of ducks on the property. "Ask for bread for the ducks."
MEMBER	California Lodging Industry Association

HOMESTEAD INN

74153 Two Mile Road, Twentynine Palms, CA 92277   *760-367-0030*

THE ROUGHLEY MANOR BED & BREAKFAST

74744 Joe Davis Road, Twentynine Palms, CA 92277   *760-367-3238*
Jan & Gary Peters, Innkeepers   *FAX 760-367-3238*
EMAIL *themanor@cci-29palms.com*
WEBSITE *www.virtual29.com/themanor*

LOCATION	Go east on Twentynine Palms Highway past the stoplight at Adobe Road to the yellow blinking light at Utah Trail. Turn left (north), go to the first cross street and turn right onto Joe Davis Road. Go 0.4 mile.
OPEN	All year
DESCRIPTION	A 1929 eastern Pennsylvania–style native-stone inn decorated with antiques and overstuffed couches and chairs, located on 25 secluded acres.
NO. OF ROOMS	Four rooms with private bathrooms and five rooms share two bathrooms. Try the Campbell Room in the main house or the Farmhouse Cottage.
RATES	Year-round rates are $125 for a single or double with a private bathroom, a suite, or a cottage, and $75-100 for a single or double with a shared bathroom. There is no minimum stay, and cancellation requires three days' notice for nonholidays, 14 days for holidays and groups.
CREDIT CARDS	American Express, MasterCard, Visa

BREAKFAST	Full breakfast is served in the dining room or on the patio and includes strawberries or bananas with cream, or a variety of fruits with a scoop of sorbet, or stuffed pears with brandy butter; a main course such as French toast with raspberry sauce, potato quiche, twice-baked potatoes topped with eggs and bacon, or gingerbread pancakes with lemon sauce.
AMENITIES	Desserts, coffee, and tea every evening in the Great Room; robes; hot tub under the stars; gazebo; Great Room will accommodate up to 32 for meetings or get-togethers; air conditioning.
RESTRICTIONS	No smoking, no pets, children OK by prior arrangement. Sara is the resident golden retriever.
REVIEWED	*Frommer's Wonderful Weekends from Los Angeles, Southern California: Romantic Weekends*
MEMBER	California Lodging Industry Association

VENICE

Just south of Santa Monica and adjacent to Marina del Rey on Highway 1, Venice is the home of "Muscle Beach," the bodybuilding capital of Southern California. Check out the amazing murals that adorn Venice's public buildings. The ocean-front walkway is a favorite focal point for local filmmakers. Stop in and see first-hand the musicians, magicians, jugglers, bodybuilders, skaters, and others who crowd the boardwalk and give Venice its unique personality.

VENICE BEACH HOUSE

15 30th Avenue, Venice, CA 90291   *310-823-1966*
Betty Lou Weiner, Innkeeper   *FAX 310-823-1842*
WEBSITE *www.travelguides.com/inns/full/CA/1817.html*

OPEN	All year
DESCRIPTION	An elegant, historic 1911 beach house.
NO. OF ROOMS	Nine rooms, four with private bathrooms.
RATES	Year-round rates are $85-165 for a double. Call for cancellation information.
CREDIT CARDS	American Express, MasterCard, Visa
BREAKFAST	Continental plus is served.
AMENITIES	Sitting room, rose garden, piano, fireplaces.
RESTRICTIONS	No smoking, no pets, no handicapped accessibility, children are welcome.

VENTURA

Two good reasons to visit Ventura are the city's outstanding beaches, especially those at Point Mugu State Park, and its position as the portal to the Channel Islands, "America's Galapagos," 15 miles offshore. In town, explore the Old San Buenaventura historic area. Ojai, the artist's colony, is an easy drive from here. Ventura is off Highway 101, 30 miles south of Santa Barbara, just north of the Los Angeles sprawl.

BELLA MAGGIORE INN

67 S California Street, Ventura, CA 93001   805-652-0277
Thomas J. Wood, Innkeeper   800-523-8479
WEBSITE travelguides.com/inns/full/CA/1860.html   FAX 805-648-5670

OPEN	All year
DESCRIPTION	A large inn decorated with antiques, chandeliers, and original artwork.
NO. OF ROOMS	Twenty-four rooms with private bathrooms.
RATES	Please inquire about current rates and cancellation information.
CREDIT CARDS	American Express, Diners Club, Discover, MasterCard, Visa
BREAKFAST	Full breakfast is served.
AMENITIES	Handicapped accessibility, wine and snacks in the evening, sitting room, sun deck, conference room, piano, spas in some rooms, garden courtyard, champagne for honeymoons and anniversaries, ceiling fans, some rooms with air conditioning, off-street parking, a close walk to the beach
RESTRICTIONS	No pets, children are welcome.

LA MER BED & BREAKFAST

411 Poli Street, Ventura, CA 93001   805-643-3600
Michael & Gisela Baida, Innkeepers   888-223-0068
German and Spanish spoken   FAX 805-653-7329
WEBSITE www.vcol.net/lamer

LOCATION	From Los Angeles, take Highway 101 north to the California Street exit, drive 3 blocks to Poli Street, turn left, and go half a block. Coming from the north, exit Highway 101 at Main Street, drive 1 mile to Oak Street, turn left, and go 1 block to Poli.
OPEN	All year

DESCRIPTION	An 1890 two-story Victorian Cape Cod decorated with antiques and European themes, overlooking the California coastline.
NO. OF ROOMS	Five rooms with private bathrooms.
RATES	Year-round rates are $115-185 for a single or double. There are midweek discounts and group rates available. There is a two-night minimum stay on weekends from March through October and holiday weekends from November through February. Cancellation requires seven days' notice.
CREDIT CARDS	American Express, MasterCard, Visa
BREAKFAST	Bavarian breakfast includes fresh orange juice, fresh fruit, muesli, cheese, Black Forest ham, European breads, breakfast cakes, croissants, and coffee.
AMENITIES	Complimentary bottle of wine, one room with wood-burning stove, picnic baskets, therapeutic massage, on-site parking.
RESTRICTIONS	No smoking, children over 10 are welcome. There are a resident pooch, a cat, 20 doves, and four hens on the property.
RATED	AAA 2 Diamonds

VISALIA

The gateway to Sequoia and Kings Canyon National Parks, Visalia is 6 miles east of Highway 99 at the junction of Highways 63 and 198.

BEN MADDOX HOUSE

601 North Encina Street, Visalia, CA 03291
Diane Muro, Innkeeper
EMAIL *muro@lightspeed.net*
WEBSITE *benmaddoxhouse.com*

559-739-0721
800-401-9800
FAX 559-625-0420

LOCATION	A half mile north of Highway 198 at the Central Visalia exit.
OPEN	All year
DESCRIPTION	A restored 1876 Victorian vernacular inn with early American decor set on half an acre in the historic district. Listed on the State Historic Register.
NO. OF ROOMS	Four rooms with private bathrooms. Try the Ben Maddox Room.
RATES	Year-round rates are $70-125 for a single or double. There is a minimum stay on major holidays, and cancellation requires 72 hours' notice.
CREDIT CARDS	American Express, Discover, MasterCard, Visa

BREAKFAST	Full breakfast is served in the dining room, on the deck, or in the gardens. Guests select from a menu.
AMENITIES	Cable TV with movie channels, private telephone lines with data ports, sherry in rooms, swimming pool, air conditioning.
RESTRICTIONS	No smoking, no pets, children over 10 are welcome.
REVIEWED	*The Official Guide to American Historic Inns, Breakfast in Bed Cookbook, Frommer's*
MEMBER	California Association of Bed & Breakfast Inns, Professional Association of Innkeepers International, Sequoia Bed & Breakfast Association
RATED	AAA 3 Diamonds
AWARDS	1996, Annual Beautification Award, City of Visalia

SPALDING HOUSE

631 North Encina Street, Visalia, CA 93291   559-739-7877
WEBSITE *www.quikpage.com/S/spaldinghouse*   FAX 559-625-0602

OPEN	All year
DESCRIPTION	A restored 1901 colonial revival host home decorated with antiques, oriental rugs, and accents from Williamsburg.
NO. OF ROOMS	Three suites with private bathrooms.
RATES	Year-round rates are $75-85 for a single or double. There is no minimum stay, and cancellation requires 24 hours' notice.
CREDIT CARDS	MasterCard, Visa
BREAKFAST	Full gourmet breakfast is served in the dining room.
AMENITIES	Music room with a piano, library, sitting room with TV and games.
RESTRICTIONS	No smoking indoors, no pets.

WOODLAKE

In the foothills of the Sierra Nevada mountains, Woodlake is about 20 miles from the southwest entrance to Sequoia National Park. Lovely Lake Kaweah is about a dozen miles to the east.

WICKY UP RANCH BED & BREAKFAST

22702 Avenue 344, Woodlake, CA 93286   559-564-8898
Monica & Jack Pizura, Innkeepers   FAX 559-564-3981
EMAIL wickyupBB@aol.com   WEBSITE www.wickyup.com

OPEN	All year
DESCRIPTION	A 1902 two-story Craftsman-style host home decorated with cedar accents, antiques, and original art.
NO. OF ROOMS	Two rooms with private bathrooms. Choose the Harding Room.
RATES	Year-round rates are $70-90 for a single or double. Cancellation requires seven days' notice.
CREDIT CARDS	No
BREAKFAST	Full breakfast is served in the dining room by candlelight or on the garden patio and includes homemade treats and fresh-squeezed orange juice.
AMENITIES	Social hour on the veranda or by the fireplace, piano, fresh flowers, robes, gardens, in-room massage.
RESTRICTIONS	No smoking inside, no pets
KUDOS/COMMENTS	"A feeling of paradise...such romance...such charm"

YUCAIPA

OAK GLEN BED & BREAKFAST

39796 Pine Bench Road, Yucaipa, CA 92399   909-797-7920

INDEX

W–Z